THE
TRADE SECRETS
HANDBOOK:

**Strategies and Techniques for
Safeguarding Corporate Information**

DENNIS UNKOVIC

PRENTICE-HALL, INC.

ENGLEWOOD CLIFFS, NEW JERSEY

Prentice-Hall International, Inc., *London*
Prentice-Hall of Australia, Pty, Ltd., *Sydney*
Prentice-Hall Canada, Inc., *Toronto*
Prentice-Hall of India Private, Ltd., *New Delhi*
Prentice-Hall of Japan, Inc., *Tokyo*
Prentice-Hall of Southeast Asia Pte, Ltd., *Singapore*
Whitehall Books, Ltd., Wellington, *New Zealand*
Editora Prentice-Hall do Brasil Ltda., *Rio de Janeiro*
Prentice-Hall Hispanoamericana, S.A., *Mexico*

Library of Congress Cataloging in Publication Data

Unkovic, Dennis
    The trade secrets handbook.

    Includes index.
    1. Trade secrets—United States.   I.   Title.
HD38.7.U55   1985   658.4'72   84-26333

ISBN 0-13-925926-0

Printed in the United States of America

To My Wife Diane

ACKNOWLEDGMENTS

My deepest appreciation to my partner, Kenneth G. Judson, for his invaluable assistance in helping to refine the book into its present form. Thanks also to James M. Sander for his research efforts.

Thanks to Sarah McAuliffe, Helen Klein and Bob Wenzel for typing, revising, and processing the multiple drafts of the manuscript.

Introduction

If you are a top executive and responsible for the day-to-day operations of a business, this book is for you. This is *not* a book for lawyers. You will learn that the best existing method to protect most valuable corporate information is by trade secrets, not patents and copyrights. A clear understanding is needed of what trade secrets are and how they affect the long-term viability of companies. In short, trade secrets are the key to corporate survival.

Trade secrets have tremendously broad applications. They are not merely suitable for protecting the trade secret formulation of *Coca-Cola®* or a proprietary manufacturing process. Many things thought of as common and not unusual can be valuable corporate trade secrets such as: the test results from unsuccessful experiments, lists of existing customers, present and proposed corporate marketing strategies, technological planning documents, information relating to the reliability of products, financial projections for the profitability of operating units, the lists of component suppliers to your company or sources of raw materials, the identity of your company's agents and distributors, and your corporate correspondence relating to non-public issues. The list is endless. Essentially, anything can be a trade secret if you treat it as secret and carry out reasonable efforts to shield it from your competitors.

Do not make the mistake of thinking that trade secrets are a concern only for high-tech companies. All companies, regardless of their size or dependence upon technology, possess valuable trade secrets. Unfortunately, too many businesses overlook the importance of trade secrets until they are confronted with a real problem. This book presents practical solutions to real life problems.

While trade secret disputes rarely reach the front pages of the business section, cases which are reported underscore the critical importance of trade secrets. A widely reported incident was the Hitachi/IBM controversy. According to published reports, Hitachi attempted to purchase critical IBM design formulations without IBM's consent. Had IBM's trade secrets been successfully pirated, the long-term implications would have been incalculable. This is not to suggest that only large companies are at risk. Frequently, small companies with a few key trade secrets that allow them to be competitive are most hurt when secrets are stolen. This book adopts the posture of a company that wants to keep its trade secrets, large and small, out of the hands of competitors.

Chapter One explains the reasons why patents and copyrights which were the traditional methods of protecting corporate information are less valuable today than ever before. While patents are not totally outmoded, trade secrets are a superior method to shield most corporate information from competitors for many reasons.

It is critical to know what trade secrets are without consulting a lawyer. Chapter Two precisely examines the meaning of trade secrets, corporate information and know-how in a manner directed at the corporate executive. It shows where to look to locate and isolate corporate trade secrets.

A formalized trade secret protection program is a must for every company. Chapter Three tells who is best qualified to set up a corporate trade secret program. It sets forth a workable plan on how to locate, indentify, and categorize trade secrets within your company.

The greatest threat to any company's trade secrets comes from present or former employees. While much is written about widespread corporate espionage by outsiders, most stolen trade secrets are taken by employees who at one time have had authorized access to those secrets. Chapter Four recommends specific pre-employment screening procedures, techniques for dealing with your employees during their term of employment, and ways to react to the employee who leaves. The employee secrecy agreement is the centerpiece of trade secret protection. Chapter Four offers practical advice on how to deal with employees whom you suspect of stealing trade secrets.

A major risk to your trade secrets comes from those outsiders to whom you reveal trade secrets for some good reason. Consultants, lawyers, subcontractors, suppliers, bankers, and even members of your board of directors can endanger trade secrets. Chapter Five tells how to limit the risks posed by outsiders. The secrecy agreement designed to bind outsiders is an important element in the strategy and is examined at length.

Perhaps the predominant method by which information is exchanged worldwide today is through licensing. Chapter Six presents the perspective of a company which desires to license its trade secrets. The licensing of trade secrets is broken into five separate stages: locating and evaluating potential licensees; the pre-negotiation secrecy agreement; negotiating a workable trade secret license; the key elements contained in a trade secret licensing agreement; and how to protect trade secrets during the life of the license. The chapter's step-by-step analysis should help both experienced licensors and the inexperienced newcomer to deal more effectively in licensing trade secrets.

Chapter Seven tackles an equally complex topic—trade secrets and joint ventures. It addresses the real concerns of a company that is obligated to reveal its trade secrets to its joint venture partners. The potential pitfalls to trade secrets created by joint ventures and practical solutions appear throughout this comprehensive analysis.

While some companies are capable of handling their trade secrets within the United States, the same companies frequently run into serious problems when transacting business internationally. Numerous obstacles can affect the use of trade secrets outside the United States—some result from the application of United States laws, others from foreign jurisdictions and their laws. Chapter Eight begins with an overview of how the United States export control laws can act as a bar to the licensing, sale, and use of your United States trade secrets internationally. It then examines the United States antitrust laws and foreign anticompetition statutes as potential bars to trade secret uses. The status of trade secrets in the European Economic Community, Japan, and Latin American countries is used to illustrate how differently trade secrets are treated outside the United States.

While trade secrets affect all businesses, they present unique issues for high-tech companies. Chapter Nine analyzes trade secrets and high-tech ventures. It presents a profile of the high-tech employee and highlights how such employees need to be handled with care.

If the unthinkable happens and your trade secrets are stolen, you must be prepared to act quickly to stop additional losses. Chapter Ten sets out the practical steps to follow in a comprehensive trade secret protection plan. You will learn what court injunctions are and how they are helpful, the role of the courts in protecting trade secrets, and the rationale in some cases for bringing criminal actions against those who steal trade secrets.

Trade secrets are critical to all companies. Inattention can lead to disaster. This book is written to help the executive understand and then plan effectively. The corporate strategy followed in advance of when a problem arises will dictate how successful your company will be.

CONTENTS

Introduction 9

**1. Changing Realities for Protecting Corporate Information
in the 1980s** 21

The Historical Alternatives for Protecting Commercial Information from
    Competitors   23
Patents—Outmoded Tools for New Technologies?   24

> *Disclosure, Costs, and Territorial Coverage—The
> Federal Courts and Patent Validity—Speed of Technol-
> ogy Development—Patents Not Applicable to Many
> Technologies—The "World" Market for Technology
> and Innovation*

The Need to Protect Corporate Information   27
Strategy to Protect Corporate Trade Secrets   27

2. Trade Secrets—Your Corporate Dowry for Survival 31

Introduction   31
Basic Terms and Concepts   31

> *What Is a Trade Secret?—The Three Legal Elements
> That Make Up a Trade Secret—What Is Know-How?—
> What Is a Patent?—What Is a Copyright?*

Items Your Company Should View as Trade Secrets   41
How Our Courts View Trade Secrets and Confidentiality   44
Which Option Is Best: Trade Secrets or Patents and Copyrights?   45

**3. A Practical Strategy to Identify and Protect Corporate
Trade Secrets** 47

Why You Need a Program to Identify and Protect Corporate
    Trade Secrets   49
Whom Should Your Company Use to Set Up a Trade Secret
    Protection Program?   49
Stage One—Locating, Identifying, and Categorizing Corporate
    Trade Secrets   50

> *How to Locate Trade Secrets—Five Areas of Evalua-
> tion—How to Categorize Your Trade Secrets to Reflect
> Their Importance*

Stage Two—The Major Elements of a Corporate Trade Secret
    Protection Program   55

*The Need for Physical Isolation of Trade Secrets Within
Designated Areas—Accountability and Tracking
Custody of Trade Secrets—The Requirement of Uniform Trade Secret Marking Procedures—The Role of
Mechanical Security Procedures—Dealing with Your
Employees at Every Stage of the Relationship—Limiting Risks when Revealing Trade Secrets to Third Parties—The Need to Deal with Unsolicited Submissions
of Proprietary Information and Employee Developments—The Requirement of Periodic Updates of Corporate Trade Secret Information*

4. Your Employees—The Greatest Threat to Trade Secrets **61**

Why Employees Represent the Greatest Threat to Your Trade Secrets   63
Why Key Employees Leave Comfortable Jobs and May Take
    Trade Secrets with Them   64
How to Gauge the Potential Problems Posed by Different
    Employees   64

*The Top Executive—Clerical Personnel—High-Level
Research Personnel—Technical and Engineering Sup-
port Personnel—Corporate Planning and Marketing
Employees—Financial and Operational Employees—
Custodial Staff*

The Need for Pre-Employment Screening Procedures   67

*What Role Will Trade Secrets Play in the Activities of a
Potential Employee?—Evaluating the Prospective Employee—The Employment Interview and Presentation
of Corporate Policy on Trade Secrets*

How to Deal with Employees and Trade Secrets During the Term
    of Employment   70

*The Requirement of an Employee Secrecy Agreement—
Mandated Employee Educational Updates—How to
React to the Employee Suspected of Stealing Trade
Secrets*

How to React when Your Employee Announces He Is Leaving   75

*The Employee Exit Interview—The Post-Employment
Consultation Relationship—Periodic Employment Update Checks*

5. Binding the Non-Employee to Protect Your Trade Secrets **79**

How the Outsiders You Deal with Are a Threat to Your Trade Secrets   81

The Importance of Requiring a Third-Party Secrecy Agreement   83

> *Who Should Sign Secrecy Agreements— Eight Key Points to Include in an Outsider Trade Secret Agreement*

Techniques for Dealing with Specific Types of Outsiders   89

> *How to Approach Your Subcontractors—Trade Secrets and Your Suppliers—The Role of Bankers and Financial Institutions—The Venture Capital Lender—What to Do with Agents and Sales Representatives—Your Accountants and Auditors—An Area of Concern: Independent Consultants—Talking with Potential Licensing or Joint Venture Partners*

How to Handle the Request of an Outsider to Submit Trade Secrets to Your Company   92

Why You Must Be Cautious when Submitting Documents to the United States Government   93

6. Protecting Trade Secrets and Licensing of Technology **95**

What It Means to License Technology and Trade Secrets   97

> *Licensing Trade Secrets: The Disadvantages*

Controlling Future Technology Development by the Licensee— The "Grantback Paradox"   99

The Five Stages of the Licensing Transaction   103

Stage One: Locating Potential Licensees and Evaluating Their Suitability   103

> *Creating the Licensee Profile—Who is Most Qualified to Find Licensees?—Five-Step Procedure to Locate a Licensee*

Stage Two: The Secrecy Agreement—Pre-negotiation Requirement   112

> *Defining Proprietary Trade Secrecy Information—Who Is to Sign the Secrecy Agreement?—The Risks of the Large Corporation Licensee—Controlling the Conduct of Potential Licensees and Their Employees— Asking for Individual Secrecy Agreements—The Time Period the Secrecy Agreement Is Valid—The Licensor's Right to Injunctive Relief Against Violators—The Liquidated Damages Approach—The Procedures for Marking of Trade Secret Documents*

Stage Three: Trade Secrets and the Negotiation Process   117

*Major Non-Technical Points to Be Resolved by Nego-
tiation—Negotiations and the Technical Phase Problems—What to Do If the License Negotiations Collapse*

Stage Four: Important Concepts in the License Agreement   123

*The Whereas Clauses—The Parties to the Agreement—
Exclusivity and the Assignment of Rights—The Licensor as Consultant—The Individual Secrecy Agreement—Identification of Trade Secrets—Dealing with
Grantbacks of Technology—The Access to Licensee's
Books and Records—Cooperative Activities of Licensor and Licensee—Force Majeure and Licensing—Termination of the Licensing Agreement—The Life of
Secrecy Agreements*

Stage Five: Trade Secrets During the License Term   129

7. Joint Ventures and Trade Secrets **133**

What Is a Joint Venture?   135
How Joint Ventures Involving Trade Secrets Differ from Licensing
    Transactions   135
Eight Risks for the Trade Secret Joint Venturer   136

*The Continuing Obligation to Disclose Trade Secrets—
Employees of Your Joint Venture Partner—Third Par-
ties Dealing with Joint Venture—The After-Developed
Technologies and Trade Secrets—Non-Joint Venture
Activities—The Expanding Scope of a Joint Venture—
Creating Your Perfect Competitor—The Price of
Failure*

What You Should Know About Joint Ventures and the Antitrust Laws   140

*Antitrust and Joint Ventures Intended for Research and
Development—Antitrust and Non-Competitive Joint
Ventures—Antitrust and the Joint Venture Setup to Produce a New Product—The Influence of Foreign Antitrust Laws on a Joint Venture*

An Overview of the Stages of a Joint Venture Transaction   142

*How to Locate Potential Joint Venture Partners and
Protect Trade Secrets by a Pre-negotiation Secrecy
Agreement—Negotiating Joint Ventures*

8. Trade Secret Problems with International Contracts and Operations ... 169

The Perspective of The United States Businessman on Trade Secrets 171
Trap for the Unwary—Trade Secrets in the International Area 171

> *Trade Secrets and the Wholly Owned Foreign Subsidiary—Licensing of Trade Secrets Outside the United States—Joint Ventures and Trade Secrets in International Markets*

How the United States Export Control Laws Limit the Licensing, Sale, and Use of Trade Secrets Outside the United States 173

> *What Types of Information Are Subject to United States Export Controls?—How the United States Export Controls Work—Six Points of Practical Advice to Remember About the United States Export Control Laws*

Trade Secrets in the Common Law Countries 176
Civil Law Countries and Trade Secrets 176
Examples of How Trade Secrets Are Treated Differently Throughout the World 178

> *The European Economic Community—Japan—Latin America*

International Contracts—Points to Consider 183

> *Which Law Will Apply?—Definition of Trade Secrets—The Resolution of Disputes—The Ownership of After-Developed Technology*

Antitrust Laws and Trade Secrets Outside the United States 184

9. Unique Aspects of Trade Secrets for High-Tech Companies 187

The Nature of Trade Secrets for High-Tech Companies and Why They Are Most Sensitive 189

> *The Commercial Life of Trade Secrets for High Tech Companies—The Unavailability of Patent and Copyright Protection in Many High-Tech Ventures—The Risk of the High-Tech Employee—The Role of Marketing and Financial Information for the High-Tech Venture—The Problems of Outside Suppliers and Subcontractors—The Reality of Trade Secret Espionage for High-Tech Companies—High-Tech Companies Producing Technologies with Military Applications*

The Profile of High-Tech Companies: Are They Unique?   192

    The Youth and Mobility of High-Tech Innovators—The Bias Toward Innovation and Against Administration—The Short-Term Orientation Syndrome—The General Ignorance of the Legal Mechanisms to Protect Trade Secrets

Observations of the Rapidly Growing High-Tech Company   194

    The Phenomenon of Rapid Growth and Hiring Policies—The Reality of Outmoded Systems for Trade Secret Control—Dealing with Related Outside Parties and Trade Secrets—The Typical High-Tech Corporate Priorities: Innovation and Sale—Do All High-Tech Companies Get the Right Legal Advice?

The Impact of Joint Ventures and Licensing Opportunities for Growing High-Tech Companies   196

10. The Legal Strategy and Your Weapons to Stop Trade Secret Misuse and Theft **199**

The Philosophy of Punishing Trade Secret Violators   199
Attacking Trade Secret Theft with Litigation   202

    Preliminary Considerations—The Elements Necessary for Successful Litigation

Legal Weapons to Protect Trade Secrets—Three Basic Approaches   204

    Injunctions—Damages—Criminal Proceedings

Implementing a Trade Secret Recovery Procedure   206

    Demand Return of the Secret Information Prior to Instituting Suit—Preserving Secrecy During Litigation

Using the Injunction—The Blitzkrieg Technique   207

    Preliminary Relief: A Hypothetical Example—The Preliminary Injunction and the Temporary Restraining Order—The Permanent Injunction: How a Preliminary Injunction Becomes Permanent

Damages and Other Remedies   211

    What Damages Are and How to Prove Them—Seeking "Reasonable Royalties" for Stolen Secrets—Forcing the Misappropriator to "Disgorge" Profits—Who Pays Attorney's Fees?—What Are Punitive Damages?

The Option of Criminal Sactions   214

> *Federal and State Law Claims—RICO: Racketeer In-
> fluenced and Corrupt Organizations Act*

Index **219**

1

Changing Realities for Protecting Corporate Information in the 1980s

The increasing speed of technological developments, combined with growing worldwide competition, has radically altered the ways corporations can protect their inventions and proprietary information. Today, patents and copyrights often are either inappropriate or insufficient to keep valuable commercial information out of the hands of potential competitors. Chapter 1 explains why the choice of the trade secret route is preferable, in most circumstances, to the traditional patent and copyright approaches.

The Historical Alternatives for Protecting Commercial Information from Competitors

The dilemma facing one who develops new technologies today is no different from the way it was a hundred years ago. How is it possible to exploit technology, gain commercial superiority, and protect the technology from competitors? Searching for answers has consumed the energies of businessmen for generations.

The key is to protect corporate information. Since corporate information comes in many types and forms, a reliable method is needed so that individuals who develop new technologies can shield those new technologies from unauthorized use.

Our patent and copyright laws, as embodied in the United States Constitution, are supposed to foster and protect the creative individual. Historically, an inventor of a new machine, manufacturing process, or an idea with commercial potential would automatically file an application for protection under our patent laws. The theory of patent protection is that a full and complete disclosure of the invention is made to the general public in exchange for a defined monopoly power over the invention for 17 years. The inventor exploits his invention during the patent life. The holder of a copyright has a longer term but less substantive protection. Unfortunately, the practical protection offered by patent and copyright laws has been uneven at best.

Patents were highly prized during the Industrial Revolution of the nineteenth and early twentieth centuries. Patents on important ideas constituted an important strategic element in the development and growth of many large corporations that dominate late twentieth century life. Patents traditionally were considered valuable because products had a commercial life of long duration. The life of the product often exceeded the life of the patent. The grant of a 17-year patent monopoly over a product justified the costs, effort, and disclosures required to obtain patent coverage.

This is not to say that all inventors or companies in the past have tried to protect valuable information by seeking patent protection. Patenting demands full disclosure of technology. The possibility of reverse-engineering a patented product or process by a competitor represents a genuine risk that has always had to be evaluated. The problems surrounding disclosure have led some companies to implement a corporate strategy favoring trade secret protection over patenting. For over one hundred years, state courts and legislatures have developed bodies of law granting trade secrets clear levels of protection if trade secrets are properly handled by the owner. The best advantage of a trade secret over a patent is that as long as the trade secret is kept confidential, it never has to become part of the public domain. The chemical formulation for *Coca-Cola*® is one of the best examples of a trade secret. The exact formula for *Coca-Cola*® has always been a trade secret and never patented. As long as it is kept a secret, *Coca-Cola*® will never have a competitor selling exactly the same product. Had the *Coca-Cola*® formula been patented, it would by now have been part of the public domain for more than 50 years.

Since World War II, a new reality has emerged for individuals and companies. The speed at which new ideas and technologies are created today and then one after another replaced by even newer innovations is significant. For example, a computer software program may have a commercial life of only 18 months, not 18 years. The effect of accelerated technological development and the obsolescence of existing ideas on patenting is only beginning to be appreciated. Today's business executive should question seriously whether or not patents will continue to maintain their traditional importance for most companies.

Patents—Outmoded Tool for New Technologies?

There are five factors which suggest traditional patent protection may be obsolete for many of the products, processes, and inventions now emerging. The modern executive must understand those factors if he hopes to make the correct corporate decision on whether or not to patent.

Patents—Disclosure, Costs, and Territorial Coverage

The right to seek a patent is guaranteed by the United States Constitution. Underlying the theory of obtaining a patent is the duty of the applicant to make a complete public disclosure of technology in exchange for a limited monopoly. Extensive information on the form, quantity, quality, and degree of the product or process must be disclosed to obtain a patent. Obtaining a patent is expensive and time-consuming. There is little or no chance that a patent of any significant complexity can be filed and issued in less than 30 months even if all reasonable efforts to reduce the delays are taken and assuming no major problem exists in the patent application itself.

Because United States companies are competing in a world economy, patenting many types of new technology in just the United States will not make sense. The patent costs are multiplied by the number of countries where markets exist for the technology. If a patent is filed in the United States and a company then fails to obtain that patent protection in other foreign markets, competitors will produce similar products. Many foreign patents also have yearly maintenance fees which have to be paid to keep the patent in force. This can be a substantial cost to a company with a large portfolio of patents. These facts result in a basic question: How much are you willing to spend and how long are you willing to wait for the coverage a patent provides? As costs rise, the question becomes ever more difficult to answer.

The Federal Courts and Patent Validity

The treatment United States federal district court trial judges and juries give the patent once it is issued further undercuts the value of patenting. In the last two decades we have witnessed increasing numbers of patent lawsuits brought by patent owners against those they accused of patent infringement. Defendants in patent infringement cases usually argue the patent itself is invalid and therefore should be thrown out by the federal court. More than one-half of the United States patents whose validity has been challenged over the last 20 years have been held invalid in whole or in part by federal courts. This startling situation has not been lost on inventors or companies. The message is clear: the time, effort, and expense to get a patent are high but after obtaining a patent there is a high risk the courts will throw out the patent as invalid anyway. This factor has led many companies to conclude that patenting of key technology and inventions should not be automatic but should be closely evaluated *before* it is undertaken. The costs, benefits, and risks have to be weighed carefully. An interesting Congressional response to this situation was the recent creation of a special federal appeals court to decide appeals of patent disputes. It will be some years before we know if this new court will have a beneficial effect on how federal judges view patents.

Speed of Technology Development

The patent monopoly of 17 years—the "deal" between the government and the patent owner in exchange for public disclosure—

is no longer as attractive as it once was. The speed of worldwide technological innovation is moving far too quickly. The commercial life of a new technology in some cases may well be less than the two to three years it will take to obtain patent protection. Time becomes a very critical factor and raises the question of patenting technologies with short commercial lives. The disclosure and costs required by patenting may not justify the limited reward. Some companies with a dominant market position file a patent application for defensive purposes only. Filing allows them to place "patent pending" on a product to scare away competitors. However, cost is still a significant factor.

Patents Not Applicable to Many Technologies

Of prime importance to the business executive is the fact that many technologies do not lend themselves to patent protection. The very nature of some technogies makes patenting impossible. Computer software, for example, was not considered to be patentable at all until a recent court decision. That case ruled that under very narrow circumstances computer software might be patentable. The copyright law is another statutory option for the creators of computer software which offers them far better prospects, but copyright coverage itself presents a unique set of problems and generally is not as valuable as patent protection where available. The fact remains that there are many types of valuable proprietary information which cannot legally be protected by either patent or copyright laws. Another method of protection is needed.

The "World" Market for Technology and Innovation

United States companies which previously operated solely from a domestic prospective are forced today to face global competition at all levels. Instantaneous worldwide communications, combined with the relatively free trade of goods between nations, have resulted in customers and potential competitors on a worldwide basis aggressively seeking technology to fuel their businesses. The drawbacks of the patent process, with its costs, delays, and limitations, has heightened the importance of licensing and joint venturing as a means to piggyback on the developments of others. The immediate opportunities for financial return create attractive options for companies which in earlier times would have sought patent protection and been satisfied with a long-term return on their research and development costs. The tendency away from patenting and toward licensing of trade secrets or participation in a joint venture by contributing trade secrets to realize a quick financial return is a reality.

The Need to Protect Corporate Information

Vast numbers of United States businessmen fail to understand the true value of the trade secrets they possess. Regardless of its size or resources, every company controls unique forms of information that would be valuable to a competitor and must be protected.

The thesis of this book is that patents and copyrights often are either inappropriate or insufficient to keep many forms of valuable commercial information out of the hands of competitors. Understanding trade secrets in a practical corporate context, recommending specific procedures to handle those trade secrets, and protecting trade secrets during transactions are vitally necessary.

Strategy to Protect Corporate Trade Secrets

There are five objectives of this book which will be covered in the various chapters and sections.

This book is written for senior executives, not lawyers. We will examine trade secrets from a practical standpoint rather than from a legal view. Initially, we will analyze the types of commercial information possessed by most companies. Since all companies have trade secrets, any company regardless of its size or business should benefit from the analysis. Throughout the book some emphasis will be placed on higher-technology companies and the vital nature of trade secrets to high-tech activities. We will then explore techniques to isolate that information which will have the greatest commerical value to a company.

STRATEGY ONE

A detailed examination of the nature of proprietary information and trade secrets follows. The point will be made again and again that trade secrets are not a high-tech issue. All companies need to know about trade secrets. The advantages of trade secret protection over patents and copyrights will be explained in terms of both theory and practical examples. Specific examples of agreements, contracts, and forms are included to give an idea of what types of documents are most appropriate. While the examples are designed to highlight points and approaches, they are not to be implemented without the aid of experienced legal counsel.

STRATEGY TWO

Unprecedented levels of corporate espionage and internal theft of corporate information are taking place throughout the United States. Cases such as the attempted theft of key trade secret information of IBM by a large Japanese company received major public exposure. Most instances, though, are either never discovered or are so potentially embarrassing to a corporation that the theft of trade secrets never becomes known to the public. Specific security measures and corporate programs to prevent theft or unauthorized appropriation of trade secrets will be examined. We will examine how the corporate employee, in many instances, represents the greatest on-going threat to any company's trade secrets. Outsiders such as bankers, accountants, subcontractors, lawyers, and consultants comprise another danger spot. Techniques for dealing with each risk will be presented.

STRATEGY THREE

There is an increasing demand for access to the trade secrets and proprietary information of companies, particularly in the high-tech area. Companies have responded by licensing technology in exchange for royalties or by getting together with one or more companies in a joint venture to carry out activities which would not be possible individually. Extensive treatment of the licensing and the joint venture options will be presented. Trade secret information must be protected at every stage of a licensing transaction or joint venture. Otherwise, it will be irrevocably lost. We will analyze licensing and joint ventures on a step-by-step basis to provide a road map for protecting trade secrets. Surprisingly, many serious errors in trade secret transfers in licenses or joint ventures involve those companies which theoretically are the most experienced in these transactions.

STRATEGY FOUR

Although this book favors the use of the trade secret option to protect corporate proprietary information, the executive must understand all the patent and copyright options available to a company. Examples appear throughout the book. The executive who lacks a clear grasp of these concepts will be forced to rely entirely upon the opinions of legal counsel.

STRATEGY FIVE

When trade secrets are or may be wrongfully appropriated, an aggressive and immediate response is absolutely critical. When confronted with the misappropriation of trade secrets, most businessmen are ignorant about the type and degree of response to use in order to minimize the damage which has already occurred. The normal procedure is to hire a lawyer and ask for an opinion. This book will show the businessman his options in advance so that he can formulate an action plan before there is a problem and be able to question and intelligently direct his legal cousel when trade secret problems arise.

2

Trade Secrets—
Your Corporate Dowry
for Survival

Protecting trade secrets must be a top priority for all companies—there is no high-tech/low-tech distinction. Corporate survival is inextricably tied to corporate trade secrets. Chapter 2 explains what trade secrets are and where you should look for them in your company. It also analyzes how our courts view corporate trade secrets in a business situation and why trade secrets differ from patents and copyrights.

Introduction

All companies possess valuable corporate information and trade secrets. This cannot be overemphasized. The extent and value of a company's trade secrets has nothing to do with whether or not a company is viewed as a "high-tech" venture. Size of a company is no factor. Even a small 20-man shop in the machine tool business which hasn't changed its mode of operation in the last 50 years will have valuable trade secrets. Corporate executives must learn to recognize that trade secrets are a critical element in corporate survival. Before proceeding any further, it is essential to understand the meaning of basic concepts such as trade secrets, know-how, patents, and copyrights.

Basic Terms and Concepts

What is a Trade Secret?

There is no universally accepted definition of what constitutes a trade secret. Laws in the United States do not originate from a single source. There is no specific federal statute on general trade secret law, so we look to legal decisions of state courts and the laws passed by state legislatures. This means laws differ from state to state. The law of New York that limits which trade secrets an employee may reasonably take with him when he leaves his employer may be totally different from the legal rights the same employee would have if he worked in California. Your company must understand the laws in each of the states in which it does business. Although trade secrets cannot be defined with great precision, this chapter will discuss in general terms how courts view them.

Begin by thinking of trade secrets as corporate assets. They are valuable and must be protected. Trade secrets can be tangible or intangible and may consist of things such as an unpatented device, a chemical formulation, non-disclosed customer information, corporate documents, or a conversation about undisclosed corporate planning strategy. What is most peculiar about trade secrets is that a valuable trade secret in one industry will not be viewed as a trade secret in another. The precise formulation used by Procter & Gamble Co. to make cookies that were hard on the outside and soft on the inside was held as a key trade secret until P&G received a United States patent on the process in 1984, while the process for making cookies by most other companies is no trade secret. A trade secret exists more in the perception of the owner than as an actual combination of elements. A trade secret can protect a broader range of information than a patent. A patent is granted only if a unique combination of elements constitutes something truly unique. A trade secret is legally protectable even if it is only valuable to its owner. If trade secrets are legally established, state and federal courts have the power to issue injunctions and to grant other relief when trade secrets are stolen or misused.

The Three Legal Elements That Make Up a Trade Secret

Although a precise definition of what constitutes a trade secret is elusive, there are common aspects. Most courts have found that a trade secret contains at least three basic elements. The elements are *novelty, value,* and *secrecy.* If your company is trying to decide whether or not something should be viewed as a trade secret, place the corporate document or corporate information against the three criteria of novelty, value, and secrecy. This simple test can be performed by lawyers and non-lawyers. The conclusions are usually the same in any case.

Element One: A Trade Secret Has Novelty

First ask whether or not something has "novelty." Novelty refers to the nature of the information or document. If your company has had its technical staff compile from an encyclopedia a list of readily available chemical processes in one data format, that list would not be viewed by a court as being novel. To possess "novelty" in a trade secret sense, the information or process need not be totally unique, but it cannot be commonplace and readily available to anyone outside your company. Using the term novelty in a trade secret sense may be confusing to a person with knowledge of patents. Novelty is a prerequisite to obtaining a patent and novelty for patenting requires that an idea must be so unique as to be highly valuable and reduced to practice for the first time by the inventor. That level of sophistication or degree of complexity of the novelty in a patent sense is not applicable to trade secrets.

Element Two: A Trade Secret Has Value

A trade secret must also have *value*. Examine value from two perspectives. First, commercial information which enables your company to save money or to compete more effectively in the market place than you would otherwise has "value" in a trade secret sense. For example, if a company manufactures printers' ink and discovers that inks when mixed at a particular temperature become more stable, this discovery possesses a "value." The other perspective from which to view value is to examine whether a company has expended money or resources to obtain or develop commercial information it views as a trade secret. However, this is not to suggest that where an improvement on a product is discovered by accident the discovery lacks value. Once an accidental discovery has occurred, the question to ask is, whether your company would have spent money to secure the same information. An affirmative answer means the accidental discovery is valuable.

Another way to look at value is by evaluating the information and deciding if it is something competitors would want to own. Willingness of a competitor to expend resources to own it is a reflection of its value. This analytical approach is particularly applicable where your company possesses corporate information and for good business reasons decides not to exploit it. For example, an invention by an oil industry company to produce gasoline from water might be suppressed for business reasons, yet its worth is inescapable. A conscious decision not to use information, therefore, does not denigrate its "value" in a legal sense.

Element Three: A Trade Secret Must Have Secrecy

The single most important element of a trade secret is "secrecy." A trade secret is much like the classic fable of Pandora's Box. While in the box and not generally available, the information is worth protecting from competitors. Once the box is opened and if the information is voluntarily relinquished, the law states the trade secret loses its character and as a result courts will no longer legally protect it. The trick is to create a reasonable envelope of secrecy around trade information and yet maintain enough flexibility so that it can be commercially exploited. Numerous lawsuits have revolved around the question of whether a company kept its information secret. Most courts have said total secrecy is not required in order to maintain a legal envelope of protection.

There are three distinct situations to watch out for when handling trade secrets. First, secrecy procedures within your own company are needed to maintain confidentiality of valuable secrets among existing employees. Second, care must be taken to control when, how, and why your secrets are revealed to third parties such as subcontractors, suppliers, consultants, and financial institutions. Third, you must be prepared to deal with the difficult problem of the necessity to reveal trade secrets when a license or joint venture is contemplated. In either case, at least some information has to be shown if a deal is to be consummated. Different approaches are needed in each circumstance.

The need for secrecy within your corporation

It is necessary to maintain adequate secrecy safeguards within your company if you are to claim trade secret status for important information. You must establish proper mechanisms so that employees are aware of the absolute necessity to keep key information secret. At a minimum, your company must secure trade secret information in your files. The goal is for it to be impossible for a competitor or anyone else to get access to the trade secrets during the ordinary course of business. A common threat to trade secrets comes from a company's in-house sales force. In order to close a deal, salesmen are tempted to say more than they should. Unwittingly, they will show to potential customers documents or information which are valuable trade secrets and should not be disclosed. In the case of trade shows, conventions, and promotional campaigns there is continual interaction with customers and competitors. The human tendency is to tell too much to gain the upper hand or to exhibit superiority. These are dangerous situations for trade secrets. Frequently, companies have irretrievably lost valuable trade secrets through thoughtless actions.

Approaches must be developed to cover all possible combinations. Later chapters will examine in greater detail the following general rules:

Do not allow all employees equal access to trade secrets.

Restrict disclosure of trade secrets to selected employees who have a genuine reason to know what they contain.

Require key employees to sign individual secrecy agreements making them personally liable for unauthorized disclosures. This can have both psychological and legal advantages.

Set up a system to mark those documents and items which are considered trade secret information.

Categorize trade secrets according to importance and how they are to be handled.

Place trade secrets in secure depositories and limit access to them.

Establish employee educational programs on trade secrets. They should be conducted on a periodic basis.

Conduct pre-employment and post-employment interviews of employees. Reinforce the need to keep matters secret.

Have internal security procedures, including periodic audits and employee reviews.

Prepare a legal action plan which is ready to be implemented if trade secrets are wrongfully appropriated by employees.

Make sure your employees know about the personal risks they run if they violate the secrecy procedures.

Your company may decide to implement some or all of these suggestions to maintain secrecy within your operation. If your trade secrets are stolen or threatened with unlawful appropriation, your company must be able to demonstrate it has followed an active trade secret program if it expects a court to support a law suit. The key is to show that "secrecy" of corporate information has been a corporate goal.

The need for secrecy when revealing corporate information to outside parties

Another aspect of secrecy involves dealing with non-employees outside your company. Commercial reality often dictates that trade secrets are needed by parties who are not your employees. As a general rule, the law says a trade secret holder must prove disclosures of its trade secrets were necessary and done in an appropriate fashion. The degree of disclosure and the control exercised are key legal elements. For example, if your company manufactures a computer disc drive made up of components manufactured by a trade secret process, it may be desirable at some point to hire a subcontractor to make the component. The subcontractor will need access to relevant trade secrets. Since the disclosure is within the scope of a reasonable business activity, the disclosure itself will not disqualify the legal "secret" aspect of the information. However, you must be sure there are adequate protections to guarantee that your trade secrets are not disclosed by the subcontractor without your authorization. There are various ways to accomplish this. You may require: your subcontractor to execute a confidential disclosure agreement; employees of the subcontractor to execute individual secrecy agreements; a provision for on-site supervision by your people during the subcontractor's manufacturing operation; a periodic audit of the subcontractor's operations; or your subcontractor to post a bond guaranteeing that information will be kept secret. There is no magic formula, but what is absolutely necessary is a conscious corporate effort to maintain the secrecy at the time of disclosure and while it is used by a third party. The same techniques can be used when dealing with accountants, consultants, bankers, lawyers, and anyone else who has legitimate needs for your trade secrets.

Dealing with the general public is different. Your company must be careful not to walk into situations where your trade secrets are carelessly or unwittingly disclosed to the public. Even an unintentional disclosure could potentially disqualify your legal right to claim protection for your trade secrets in court. The legal implications are drastic since the property becomes freely available to the general public.

The need for secrecy in licensing of technology and joint venture activities

Techniques to maintain secrecy of information are critical when you contemplate transferring trade secrets to another company by means of a license, taking part in a joint venture to which your trade secrets will be contributed, or when planning an outright sale of trade secrets. While an extensive discussion of licensing and joint ventures follows in later chapters, the key point to be emphasized here is that as long as the disclosure of the trade secrets is limited and for a particular purpose, neither the licensing nor the use of trade secrets by a joint venture will violate the legal enforceability of those trade secrets. The risks arise with indiscriminate or unguarded disclosure. Similarly, the sale of trade secrets to another will not violate secrecy. By concluding the sale, you pass the torch of secrecy to the purchaser who is obligated to maintain the trade secrets and keep others from using them without permission. There remains an implied obligation on the part of the seller to preserve the confidential nature of trade secrets, even after they are sold.

In conclusion, a trade secret can be just about anything which has genuine commercial value, possesses at least some novelty that is non-public, and retains its "secret" character by the conscious efforts of the trade secret owner.

What Is Know-How?

Know-how is a sort of distant cousin to trade secrets. Applying the three criteria of novelty, value, and secrecy described earlier helps in drawing the line between what is know-how and what is a trade secret. While know-how does have genuine value to a corporation, it may not be novel or unique. Know-how is best described as information developed or accumulated by a business which is helpful in the operation of the business. Know-how is not as critically important to corporate activity as are trade secrets. For this reason, employees are normally not as strictly regulated in how they handle know-how as they would if working with their employer's trade secrets.

An example may be helpful. Let us assume a company has a continuous casting operation for high-quality steel part production. A specific machine used in the line could be a trade secret if its design were proprietary. The exact mixture of materials to form the proper steel slurry might be a trade secret. However, the floor layout for the equipment would more likely be know-how as would the best times materials should be introduced into the process. An hourly employee who worked with the continuous casting operation for years and from his experience developed a keen understanding of the best ways to maximize productivity of a continous caster would possess valuable know-how.

Due to the close relationship between know-how and trade secrets, this and the following chapters will talk only about trade secrets and it will be assumed know-how is included within trade secrets. The bottom line is the same. Your company must learn to apply the same techniques to shield valuable trade secrets and know-how from outsiders.

What Is a Patent?

Patents are more restrictive and legally demanding than trade secrets. A patent is an official grant of rights from the United States government to an inventor of a uniquely valuable commercial idea. A patent is a legal license to prevent others from making, selling, copying, or using an invention for a period of 17 years. After the patent period expires, the invention becomes part of the public domain and anyone can make, sell, or use it. An underlying public policy exists to encourage inventors to make their inventions available to the general public. A government's willingness to issue a patent granting an inventor a limited monopoly over his invention is the deal given in exchange for allowing the invention to become public property.

In order to receive a patent, an inventor must prove his invention is novel, non-obvious, and a genuine advance in the state of the art in a particular field. It is not possible to get a patent on a method of doing business, printed materials, a suggestion or non-specific idea, or an invention involving nuclear weapons. This means there are many types of valuable corporate information which could never be protected by our patent laws. Patents are normally given for new products, processes, or significant improvements over existing technologies. Once granted, a patent is like any other kind of property and it may be sold, licensed, assigned in whole or part, bequeathed in an estate, or even mortgaged. The patent law gives patent holders certain legal rights in federal courts to seek injunctions and damages when others wrongfully infringe on the patented product or process.

Even if patenting is a possibility for a particular corporate trade secret, there are some distinct disincentives. Patents are costly from the standpoint of time and legal expense. It is unusual for a patent to be granted in less than 24 months from the date an application is filed with the United States Patent Office. If an inventor feels his idea has commercial value beyond the territorial limits of the United States, he must file for a patent in those countries where protection is desired. With the quickly expanding world market for products, accurately guessing at the time an invention is first developed where it stands the best chances for sale is difficult. Unfortunately, inventors have a short time period in which to make the decision of where to patent. Also, the cost of patenting something in every major industrial country throughout the world is prohibitive except for very large companies. Even large multinationals tend to be selective about where they file for patent protection.

The dilemma facing inventors and major corporations today is the rapid speed at which technological inventions bypass each other. Fifty years ago, the commercial life of an invention could reasonably be expected to outlast the 17-year patent protection period. Today, new technologies and inventions can be outmoded within two to three years in some industries. This reality leads more and more companies to ask the question whether or not the costs and disclosures required to obtain a patent are worth the effort. Many companies have decided that the trade secret route better meets their needs.

What Is a Copyright?

A copyright is entirely distinct and different from a patent. A right guaranteed by the United States Constitution, a copyright is available to authors of literary, dramatic, musical, artistic, and other kinds of intellectual works. A copyright will protect the physical manifestation of a particular document or work of art and gives the author exclusive right to publish, print, distribute, copy, or perform it. The act of copyrighting applies not to just works of art, but also to photographs, pictorial illustrations, product labels, business books, technical manuals, advertising and sales literature, and most business-related information that is in tangible form. Recently, copyrights have received a great deal of public attention due to the efforts of some high-tech companies and individuals to copyright computer software.

It is important to stress that a copyright cannot prevent some-one from independently working toward the same result. While this specific book on trade secrets is copyrighted and may not be directly reproduced without the copyright holder's permission, anyone is free to write on the topic of trade secrets as long as the ideas are his or her own and not a mirror image of this book. This is the major difference between patenting and obtaining a copyright. While a copyright certainly provides some limited legal protection for authors, for most businesses the value of the protection available under a copyright is highly questionable if a business executive seeks to keep corporate information away from competitors. Copyrighting demands disclosure and that is the exact opposite of what businesses desire.

Items Your Business Should View as Trade Secrets

Begin by thinking of trade secrets as corporate information embodied in tangible form. Your own company's trade secrets could be a physical improvement on a machine, an industrial formulation, customer-related documents, blueprints, drawings, or vital correspond-ence. The following examples are meant only to illustrate the scope of trade secrets and should not be considered an all-inclusive list. Chapter Three will discuss in detail a definite procedure to identify your com-pany's trade secrets.

PRODUCTS

An unpatented product which is commercially valuable and has been developed or obtained by your company may be a trade secret unless it has been patented. Even if the product itself is not a trade secret, the combination and construction of its elements could be a trade secret.

FORMULATIONS

Industrial formulations are a common form of trade secret. The formulation and chemical makeup of numerous food products are valuable trade secrets. The exact ingredients and percentages or contents of cosmetics are trade secrets.

INDUSTRIAL PROCESSES

The combination of various pieces of equipment which, when operated together, form an extremely efficient industrial process may be a trade secret. The example of the production of high-quality steel by the continuous casting process was mentioned earlier. Although the production of steel by the continuous casting process is no trade secret in itself, the combination of equipment, the quality of raw materials, and the temperatures at which steps are completed is a genuine trade secret. Patenting the process would probably not be feasible. From the standpoint of disclosure required to patent, keeping the process a trade secret is a more logical way to go.

MACHINERY AND MODIFICATIONS

A piece of machinery purchased in the ordinary course of business on the open market is not a trade secret. However, the modification of a machine by your company in a unique manner to increase its productivity or usefulness could be a trade secret.

RESEARCH AND DEVELOPMENT DOCUMENTATION

How and what your company documents in its research and developmental activities may be a trade secret. Blueprints, drawings, computer-generated data, test results, and designs that are physical manifestations of the development process are examples. Even documents and records of failed efforts can properly be viewed as trade secrets. Their commercial value to the corporation is reflected in the fact that they document unsuccessful results. If a competitor were to have access to documentation of unsuccessful tests, the competitor could avoid the time or effort your company expended to reach the same conclusion.

CORRESPONDENCE

All corporate correspondence is not trade secret material. Simple transmittal letters of corporate information are not protectable. Specific correspondence, though, which relates in some way to the operations or activities of your company and could be helpful to a competitor may be viewed as a trade secret.

INTERNAL CORPORATE DOCUMENTS

Every company possesses documentation important to varying aspects of its operations. For example, to the extent corporate documents from a purchasing department show the actual cost of procuring vital goods or services, those documents can provide an insight to a competitor of how your company must price certain products. Therefore, these documents would fall into the realm of trade secrets. If your company has developed unique procedures for marketing raw materials, the marketing plans or distribution techniques could be a trade secret. Computerized printouts of inventory on hand at any given time can be a trade secret. The underlying question to be asked in each case is—what value would the document have for your competitor?

CUSTOMER INFORMATION

Information relating to customers is a fertile area for trade secrets. If your company indiscriminately sells products to any source as long as the price is acceptable, a list of your customers would probably not be a trade secret. However, in industries where the identity of customers is guarded corporate information and the ability to identify particular customers would aid competitors, customer lists in most jurisdictions are viewed as a potential trade secret.

FINANCIAL AND ACCOUNTING INFORMATION

Internal financial and accounting information, unless made publicly available, may fall under the trade secret umbrella. Even a banking relationship can be a trade secret. For example, when T. Boone Pickens made his unsuccessful attempt to take over Gulf Oil

Corporation in 1984, Pickens required advance arrangements with financial institutions for the massive lines of credit needed for a takeover bid. The identity of those banks and the credit lines they would make available were genuine trade secrets of Mesa Petroleum until the announcement of his intent became public.

LEGAL ISSUES

Threatened litigation (non-public) may have an impact on the performance of a company and should be viewed as a trade secret before the threat becomes publicly known.

PLANNING AND STRATEGY DOCUMENTATION

Long-term corporate planning, internal operation, and marketing strategy documents are trade secrets if your corporation works to maintain their confidentiality. It is surprising how many corporations are lax in protecting their future planning activities. Of course, once published in an annual report or made freely available to stockholders and outsiders, the documents lose their trade secret character.

How Our Courts View Trade Secrets and Confidentiality

In order to understand how judges and our courts view trade secrets, you have to appreciate the narrow and restricted way in which the law protects trade secrets. Because there is no general federal law on trade secrets, laws on trade secrets vary from state to state throughout the United States. In every trade secret case there are two conflicting policy issues judges must wrestle with. One public policy favors the protection of the developments of the inventors and corporations even if they decide to cloak their discovery by a trade secret. The hope is that by granting legal protection to inventors, society will be benefited by new discoveries and increased employment. The other public policy embodied in the law favors the philosophy that people should be free to earn a living in whatever way they choose. This theory leans toward competition as a way to encourage better products and services. Those who follow this theory do not favor keeping inventions or improvements as trade secrets. Judges, when evaluating the facts of each case, must balance these two inconsistent public policies. Not infrequently, therefore, two judges may reach opposite conclusions when confronted by the same fact situation.

When companies possessing trade secrets are careless in following procedures to maintain their trade secrets or are overreaching in demands placed on employees, judges can overlook the financial consequences created by a misappropriation of trade secrets and may side with the employee. Judges are people and by nature may favor an individual employee over the corporation if the corporation has abused its power. Every businessman should put himself in the judge's position and objectively evaluate his company's approach to trade secrets. Ask the question whether any sympathy would exist for the company's desire to protect its trade secrets over the employee's rights. In the close cases, trade secrets tend to lose out.

In the 1970s, the United States Supreme Court faced the issue of whether United States patent laws preempt and thus invalidate the existence of state trade secrets laws. Fortunately, the Court decided trade secrets laws have an independent legal existence. This confirmed the option of trade secrets or patents and copyrights. The courts leave the choice to business people. With that issue put to rest, federal and state courts have the power to uphold trade secrets by means of injunctions, damage suits, and other remedies *if* the trade secret holder can prove trade secrets were stolen or misused. Injunctions are generally issued only when it can be shown "irreparable harm" will result if the trade secrets are mishandled. Showing financial losses alone is not enough proof in most courts to have an injunction issued. In rare cases, criminal charges against trade secret thieves are a possibility. Ultimately, the relief courts are willing to provide depends on the facts of each case and how well the trade secret holder has protected trade secrets before there was a problem. If a court can be convinced an injustice has been done to the trade secret owner, the court will fashion a method to right the wrong.

Which Option Is Best—Trade Secrets or Patents and Copyrights?

To maintain a competitive edge, your company must keep corporate proprietary information out of the hands of competitors. Ironically, companies fail to appreciate that many valuable assets are contained in corporate proprietary information—not plants, equipment, and inventory. Equipment, inventory, and real estate can be replaced, but vital corporate information which is lost often can never be replaced. What is the best way, then, to protect corporate information? There are two options: trade secrets or patents and copyrights.

For significant inventions or key processes, assuming the strict requirements of United States patent statutes can be met, obtaining patent protection is an option. Aside from the financial costs and time delays, the major disadvantage of patenting is the public disclosure required in order to receive the patent. Unfortunately, the extent of information disclosed can give competitors insights that can permit reverse-engineering around the scope of the patent protection. Lesser forms of corporate information such as customer lists, know-how, marketing plans, legal, technical documents and information, and financial records are not even possible subjects for protection under the patent laws. The only legal protection for such information is by the trade secret route. The bottom line is that even if your company makes the decision to protect a narrow range of corporate information by patenting, most corporate information, if it is to be protected at all, will fall in the trade secret area. The preferable option therefore, for the 1980s and beyond will be trade secrets. How to identify, handle, and protect trade secrets at all levels is discussed in the chapters that follow.

3

A Practical Strategy to Identify and Protect Corporate Trade Secrets

Every company can benefit from a formal Corporate Trade Secret Protection Program. This chapter presents an action plan on how to identify, categorize, and protect corporate trade secrets. The practical suggestions will help any company regardless of its size or dependence upon proprietary information.

All corporations, regardless of their size or dependence upon technology, should have in place a comprehensive corporate policy to protect trade secrets. Obviously, there is no single program for protecting trade secrets that can meet the diverse needs of all companies. Company size, the importance of trade secrets to a company, and the resources which can be allocated to protect trade secrets will vary from company to company and by industrial sector. In order to present a complete picture, this chapter will assume your company does not have a trade secret program but desires to develop a comprehensive program to safeguard its trade secrets.

Why You Need a Program to Identify and Protect Corporate Trade Secrets

What specific procedures should be adopted on a permanent basis to assure continued protection of trade secrets? Mechanical security procedures, personnel policies in dealing with employees and outside third parties, methods for identification and marking trade secret documents, techniques for handling unsolicited submissions of information, and legal weapons to combat trade secret theft are all important elements. This chapter and those that follow will provide your corporation with a road map of strategies that can be modified to fit with your existing operations. Although companies in the manufacturing areas have traditionally given greater attention to protecting trade secrets, the approaches are equally applicable to companies in service-oriented businesses.

The trade secret protection program is divided into two major stages. The first stage focuses on isolating and identifying trade secrets. Many corporations have failed to identify their trade secrets. Once identified, trade secrets must be categorized for protection purposes. The second stage focuses on protecting trade secrets once they have been properly identified.

Whom Should Your Company Use to Set Up a Trade Secret Protection Program?

You must select the right person to take charge of establishing a trade secret protection program. There are only two alternatives: (i) hire an experienced outside consultant or (ii) designate an existing employee.

Where the cost is reasonable, hire an outside consultant to develop the trade secret program. The consultant is more familiar with the techniques and procedures for protecting trade secrets and should be able to more than justify his fee for services by accelerating the speed at which the project is completed. In addition to acting as an objective sounding board for ideas, the consultant can avoid the "inventing the wheel" syndrome. If your company decides to use an existing in-house employee for the project, you may still want to have an outside consultant to use occasionally when problems arise. Certain key elements of a trade secret program, such as individual secrecy agreements, may be politically sensitive within your corporate structure. The use of an outside consultant can ease problems an employee might not desire to take on.

If your company decides to select its own employee to establish a trade secret protection project, unique abilities are required. Since the underlying theme of the trade secret program is protection of trade secrets, using an employee with responsibilities in marketing or in sales will be a mistake. Sales or marketing personnel are trained to seek short-term profitability. The object of a trade secret program goes in the opposite direction—long-term corporate survival. The clash of the natural inclination for immediate sales versus secrecy of information represents difficult philosophies for anyone to reconcile. Employees chosen from the operational end of a company are generally far better suited than those trained in sales and marketing. The employee must understand the overall activities of his company and how the discreet mechanisms of production, marketing, financing, and research fit together. A technical background is helpful, but not essential. Where a technical evaluation of certain types of trade secrets is required, qualified employees from your company can be consulted for their opinions. Whoever is chosen must hold a sufficiently high rank in your company to demand, where necessary, the cooperation of *all* employees. He should have access to your top executives when policy decisions are required. Flexibility and organizational coordination are the two critical qualifications needed to be successful.

Stage One—Locating, Identifying, and Categorizing Corporate Trade Secrets

How to Locate Trade Secrets—Five Areas of Evaluation

Most organizations don't have an existing procedure for determining if something is or is not a trade secret. This makes the task of forming a corporate trade secret program difficult. Initially, the assignment of locating and identifying all trade secrets within a corporation will appear overwhelming. Where is one to start?

First, segregate all corporate information into distinct areas. Only after information has been segregated is it possible to test whether or not it should be classified as a trade secret. Technical information presents a unique problem. Simply applying the test of a trade secret—is it valuable, novel, and secret?—can be best evaluated by a technically knowledgeable person. Unless the trade secret program planner has a technical background, he should use employees experienced in the area under question. This is particularly true in technical fields where a process or operation might appear to a layman to be insignificant but in reality is a valuable trade secret. Only an expert knows for sure. This is why constant consultation is a prerequisite.

There is no magic formula for setting up categories of separate information. The five basic areas set forth below illustrate how categorization assists in the creation of a trade secret program.

Category One: Inventions, Industrial Processes, and Key Technical Information

A trade secret program must recognize a corporation's obligation to protect its own trade secrets. Begin with the informational sources most clearly deserving of trade secret status. The traditional focus of trade secret protection has been for unpatented inventions, unique products, industrial processes, and secret technical information of particular value. Most of these will be obvious to anyone, therefore, a company's top technical staff will usually be able to provide accurate lists. You should not overlook research in progress or research plans for they are genuinely significant to future inventions and processes. Difficulty may arise where highly skilled technical employees take things for granted and do not appreciate the value of that information to a competitor. Consultation with more than one person to check the evaluations and opinions of the technical staff is necessary. Determine who owns the unpatented inventions, products, processes, and key technical information. It is common for companies to use technical information or products licensed from outside persons. A trade secret program should recognize a corporation's obligation to protect the information licensed to it and to honor any and all restrictions placed on the information by the licensor.

Category Two: Technical Information and Materials

Locate valuable corporate documents such as working drawings, blueprints, designs, consolidated research materials, training manuals, and test data. To decide if the information should be accorded the status of a trade secret, ask whether the information would be of commercial value in the hands of a competitor. Questioning technical employees should help yield an insight into the value of information. However, it is a mistake to assume all technical information deserves trade secret status. Treating all information as a trade secret ultimately makes it more difficult to protect what is truly valuable.

Category Three: Marketing, Purchasing, Procurement, Customer, and Corporate Planning Information

After examining technical information, next isolate documents and tangible information which fall under the heading of marketing, corporate planning, purchasing and procurement, and customer-related information. Clearly, most companies already realize that their customer lists and business leads have trade secret potential. However, unique procurement and purchasing arrangements may be a valuable trade secret and yet go unrecognized. Definitive marketing and corporate planning strategies which reflect corporate decisions for allocating of resources are trade secrets. Since most information of this kind is non-technical, pay attention to the employees in these areas. An educational briefing is recommended so that the non-technical employee will understand that marketing, purchasing and procurement, and planning information is a trade secret. Educating the marketing and sales staff will probably require the greatest effort.

Category Four: Financial, Accounting, Legal, and Securities-Related Information

Financial information in its multiple forms is indispensable to the efficient operation of a company. Specific financial information, such as the exact budgetary allocation for development of a new product, can be a trade secret. It is an impossible task to take each piece of financial data and to classify it for trade secret purposes. A company's internal systems and the kinds of financial information they create must be identified. Interviews with the financial staff at all levels will produce an overall picture. Only then can basic decisions be made as to the trade secret restrictions which will be reasonable. For example, assume the controller and top financial staff of your company meet on a quarterly basis to project the profitability of a new operating unit in a highly competitive industry. The results of quarterly meetings in the form of written minutes, financial data, and projections could be used by a competitor to the great detriment of your company. The goal of any trade secret program is to alert employees of the overall importance of the information they generate and the specific steps to be followed in protecting the information.

Legal documents can also be trade secrets of your company. Both in-house legal staff and outside law firms representing your company should be consulted. Possible exposure to a law suit is an area which should be viewed as a trade secret because improper disclosure could be harmful to the corporation. For example, internal documents relating to an inherent defect in an automobile could have disastrous effects on an automobile manufacturer if improperly disclosed or disclosed prematurely. The risk generally does not come from the lawyers passing on information to outside parties. The real problem arises when information with legal ramifications is transmitted within a company in a haphazard manner and becomes available to employees who do not recognize their responsibility to keep the information secret. Another aspect is information relating to insider information with securities implications. The leak of a proposed merger, for example, would not only be harmful to the transaction, but could mean personal liability for the employee if state securities bureaus or the Federal Securities and Exchange Commission become involved. Again, setting parameters with a trade secret program around these situations can lessen the chance of problems.

Category Five: Other Corporate Data

Finally, an attempt should be made to examine all activities of a company, including the maintenance of its books and records. The search may disclose general systems, employment practices, or corporate policies which may be considered trade secrets. For example, if your company is in high-tech research and development, it may desire to hire research employees with specific background skills. Existing employment records may specifically reveal the depth of expertise among existing employees. This data may be a trade secret.

*How to Categorize Your Trade Secrets to
Reflect Their Importance*

After completing the time-consuming project of reviewing all types of corporate information, you will be left with a tremendous volume of information—one pile of non-trade secret information and a second pile of information of potential trade secrets. The next step is to take the mass of information with trade secret potential and rank the information by level of commercial value to your company. Failure to distinguish between types of trade secret information will undercut the value of the overall trade secret program.

Each company, depending on its size, has to establish categories that fit its needs much like the way the United States government classifies its documents by top secret, confidential limited official use, and public document. One approach is to break down confidential information categories: critical trade secrets (CTS), important trade secrets (ITS), trade secrets (TS) and know-how (K-H). By placing information in distinct areas it will be easier to decide what resources can be devoted to protecting the various levels of information.

Critical Trade Secret Information (CTS)

Virtually every company will have at least a small group of exceptionally valuable trade secrets. Unpatented industrial formulations and unpatented products are good examples. Particular care must be taken to protect these critical trade secrets (CTS). It is a mistake to admit more than a few trade secrets to this category. The more narrowly defined, the greater the opportunity to protect them.

Important Trade Secrets (ITS)

In level of descending importance, Important Trade Secrets (ITS) are very valuable, but if revealed, the result would not be catastrophic. Information such as working drawings, detailed designs of commercial products, research, working papers of developing technologies, and comprehensive internal manuals should be classified as Important Trade Secrets. Important Trade Secrets merit a high degree of attention. Again, the number of documents given this classification should be limited in order to enhance their meaningfulness for employees who handle them.

Trade Secrets (TS)

All other documents and information that meet the three-part test of value, novelty, and secrecy should be placed in the trade secrets (TS) category. Accounting information, corporate planning documents, marketing plans, purchasing and procurement information, financial and accounting records, and correspondence of certain types are likely candidates. Normally, trade secrets in this category would be valuable to a competitor, but their disclosure would not mean an immediate irreparable harm.

Know-How (K-H)

Clearly, not all information valuable to a competitor falls under the classification of a trade secret. Training manuals, miscellaneous technical documents, selected correspondence, and customer information and preferences are probably know-how and do not rise to the level of a trade secret. Although worth protecting, they do not justify the expense of the same control mechanisms and restrictions applicable to trade secrets. Nevertheless, by identifying and isolating know-how (K-H), your company can advise employees of the confidential nature of know-how in the workplace.

Stage Two: The Major Elements of a Corporate Trade Secret Protection Program

A comprehensive trade secret program for a company can be simple or complex. The needs and resources of an enterprise will dictate how extensive a trade secret program is. There are at least eight major elements which appear in most comprehensive corporate trade secret protection programs. Each element must be evaluated when structuring a program for your company once the First Stage identification of your trade secrets is completed.

Element One: The Need for Physical Isolation of Trade Secrets Within Designated Areas

After categorizing the various levels of trade secrets and distinguishing them from know-how, physically isolate trade secrets and know-how from non-trade secrets information. At the very least, depositories for trade secrets in Critical Trade Secret (CTS) and Important Trade Secret (ITS) categories are essential.

For the company relying heavily on research and developmental activities, the information used by the engineers and researchers which qualifies trade secret coverage has to be placed in a designated area under established controls.

For large companies with multiple operating units the task is more difficult because trade secrets are present at multiple locations. Whatever the number of locations, an effective trade secret program must be able to identify where trade secrets are, which categories of trade secrets exist at each depository, and what security procedures are in effect to limit access by employees.

Element Two: Accountability and Tracking Custody of Trade Secrets

To be certain a court of law will uphold the right of your company to claim trade secret protection for specific information, you must be able to demonstrate that all reasonable efforts have been taken to keep trade secret information from being disclosed without authorization. Simply maintaining a depository for trade secrets is useless unless accountability of those employees reviewing trade secrets is set in motion. Corporate trade secret procedure has to be able to track trade secrets from the time they leave a depository until they are returned. This concept is best understood by reference to how the military handles defense secrets. Imagine a situation where nuclear research documents now in Los Alamos, New Mexico, are needed in Denver at a government research laboratory. For the period of time the research documents leave the New Mexico facility, are transported to Denver, are used by the Denver researchers, and later returned to Los Alamos, a responsible military official must be able to prove the documents were in his possession or under his control at all points in between. The documents cannot have been tampered with. Any break in the chain of custody will mean the military officer is subject to court martial, because loss of custody means the information contained in the documents may have been compromised. The law views trade secrets in the same manner. Trade secrets are protected by our courts only if a trade secret owner can prove that at every stage all reasonable efforts were made to maintain their confidential status.

Element Three: The Requirement of Uniform Trade Secret Marking Procedures

All trade secret programs require a uniform procedure for marking documents considered trade secrets. This is particularly critical for CTS and ITS trade secrets. If a chemical formulation is contained on a single piece of paper and on its face does not indicate it is a trade secret, you may not be able to keep a competitor from using it if he somehow manages to obtain it. A court may not grant you an injunction prohibiting a competitor from using the formula absent proof of a theft or a clear mark on the document. If a document is so important and valuable, a court will ask: Why didn't the corporation take the time to mark it "Trade Secret"? More specific suggestions on marking trade secret documents appear in later chapters.

Element Four: The Role of Mechanical Security Procedures

A comprehensive review of all possible mechanical or physical security procedures for trade secrets is not within the scope of this book. Mechanical procedures work on multiple levels: to restrict employee access, to limit authorized third-party use, to shield secrets from the general public, and to stop trade secret theft. Whether or not security guards, badges, locked rooms, fences, and mechanical devices limiting entry are advisable is a decision best left to professional security consultants. The importance of mechanical security procedures, though, should not be overlooked in planning a corporate trade secret program.

Element Five: Dealing with Your Employees at Every Stage of the Relationship

Employees are the major factor leading to unauthorized disclosure of trade secrets. All corporate trade secret programs must define which employees are authorized to see and use trade secrets as part of their job. Generally, the greater the degree of secrecy and commercial value, the more limited the access employees should be given. Chapter Four is exclusively devoted to analyzing how employees can be controlled and to the personnel policies and the continuing education process that are required. Employees must understand the need to maintain the confidentiality of trade secrets as a condition of employment.

Element Six: Limiting Risks when Revealing Trade Secrets to Third Parties

The operation of any business often requires that trade secrets be shown to outside parties for some legitimate reason. The outsiders may be subcontractors, suppliers, consultants, lawyers, bankers, or accountants. A corporate trade secret program must set forth the circumstances when disclosure is authorized, the scope of disclosure permitted, and those occasions when individual secrecy agreements are a prerequisite to any disclosure. For example, a trade secret program could make the hiring of an unrelated outside consultant dependent on the consultant's prior agreement to execute a secrecy agreement. While no hard and fast rules are possible, the best approach is for you to establish parameters in your corporate policy and then allow flexibility to specific individuals in your organization. Only they are authorized to make exceptions when warranted. Accountability is the key. The corporate policy must force the responsible corporate official to decide if a secrecy agreement is a prerequisite to any disclosure to an outsider. Chapter Five deals in depth with the problems and techniques of dealing with outsiders.

Element Seven: The Need to Deal with Unsolicited Submissions of Proprietary Information and Employee Developments

Part of your corporate trade secret policy must address the unsolicited submission of a trade secrets scenario. Most companies at one time or another are approached by an outside party who asks you to examine an invention or idea developed by that outsider. The outsider hopes to sell or license its technology to you. The unspoken danger in examining outside documents is that subsequently the outsider will claim its idea was stolen by your company. If you are faced with a lawsuit for damages, your company had better have procedures established beforehand. Your corporate trade secret program should define how outside ideas will be examined and what techniques are used to avoid potential liability.

Similar problems can arise with your own employees. What is a corporation to do when by way of a suggestion box or otherwise an employee submits an idea to his employer? What liability, if any, does the employer have to its employee? Or, how does a corporation handle the situation where an employee claims to have invented something on his own time? The employee may wish to sell it to his employer, to quit the company and set up his own business, or to sell his invention to another company. Most courts support claims of an employer to inventions developed by an employee during the term of employment and while at the place of employment. A corporate trade secret program and employment policy that fails to define in advance what the rights or responsibilities are of both parties is heading for trouble.

Element Eight: The Requirement of Periodic Updates of Corporate Trade Secret Information

Once your corporate trade secret program has been developed and put in place, it should operate smoothly for a certain period. With time, circumstances will change. There is a continuing need to update your company's Trade Secret Program Information on a periodic basis. The procedure cannot be a static mechanism. For example, at least every three years make an evaluation of your CTS and ITS to see if they are up to date. Almost certainly, much of what appears will be out of date. In short, it must be given constant attention and a high priority if the program is to remain effective.

Conclusion

No company has to incorporate every suggestion offered to secure its trade secrets. What is required is the recognition of the desirability of developing a simple, yet comprehensive, plan to meet the particular needs of your company. The best approach is to discard all past practices and to begin with an open mind. The following chapters will flesh out the skeleton just presented.

4

Your Employees—
The Greatest Threat
to Trade Secrets

The greatest overall threat to your company's trade secrets comes from present or former employees. This chapter outlines the steps to take at every stage to prevent unauthorized disclosure of trade secrets by employees.

Why Employees Represent the Greatest Threat to Your Trade Secrets

Most businessmen look outside of their organizations for real or imagined threats to their trade secrets and proprietary information. It is easier to accept danger from external sources than to concede that the greatest danger comes from within. Historically, however, more trade secrets have been stolen or improperly divulged by employees than by outsiders. Will the trade secrets now in the head of your employee end up in the hands of a competitor?

Access to information is the key. Employees have access to information either as part of their normal activities or by their mere physical presence within an organization. Many employees will never be questioned for looking in a file or copying a document. An employee can obtain information without the need for hidden microphones, breaking and entering, bribery, or stealth.

Disclosures by employees can cover a multitude of sins. Because employees have such easy access to information, they can jeopardize confidential corporate information through carelessness as well as through premeditated disclosure. The salesman attempting to land a new sales prospect may reveal secret aspects of a new product without realizing how valuable the secrets are to a comptetitor. A secretary may carelessly leave on her desk photocopies of trade secret documents which can be seen and copied by anyone. Research personnel, while attending a symposium, may reveal secrets in response to questions concerning new products in development. A corporate pilot may mention he is flying top executives into a small town where there is only one company of any significance. If the trips become increasingly frequent, a sharp observer might conclude an acquisition is being discussed. The pilot's indiscretions could result in the potential acquisition candidate's stock becoming inflated. Although none of these employees consciously intend to harm their employers, the damage nevertheless occurs. Careful planning and workable procedures can greatly limit these unintended disclosures.

Premeditated appropriation of an employer's trade secrets is the second way an employee can seriously harm his employer. The most common situation occurs when an ambitious employee decides to start his own business. Having easy access to the employer's trade secrets may ease the transition. Less common, but equally problematical, is the employee who for personal gain passes on your company's trade secrets to competitors. In either case, the premeditated nature of the employee's actions is difficult to predict and to control.

Why Key Employees Leave Comfortable Jobs and May Take Trade Secrets With Them

Premeditated trade secrets theft by employees is a real problem. While there is no single answer, there are at least three distinct factors that contribute to the phenomenon. The most basic is the changing attitude toward traditional employer/employee role in industry. The employer is no longer in a dominant position with key employees. It is no longer reasonable for an employee to expect or to want to spend his working lifetime with one corporation or in a particular industry. This is especially true for those with technical skills which are in demand and with multiple industry applications. The ease of mobility from job to job or between industry sectors creates a lack of permanence possible for those with skills. A second factor is the growing entrepreneurial explosion among those with technological skills. Large corporations, with a few notable exceptions, are perceived as the antithesis of creativity. The innovative don't believe their creativity will necessarily be recognized or financially rewarded by the large corporation. The last factor is a function of the availability today of many sources of venture capital. Financing a new company is much easier in the 1980's than it was 20 years ago when financing tended to come from more conservative, institutional sources of money.

The cycle becomes a self-fulfilling prophecy in that large companies needing new technologies tend to acquire new and developing companies. It is easier to buy companies than to innovate in-house. The financial possibilities are not lost upon new companies and entrepreneurs, so the mad race continues. Since these financial opportunites exist, the temptations to employees with access to trade secrets accelerate.

How to Gauge the Potential Problems Posed by Different Employees

When your company decides to create a comprehensive trade secret program, one of the first places to start is by taking a hard look at your employment procedures. Any company must develop an over-all philosophy on the importance of trade secrets and their relationship to all employees regardless of job description or level of compensation. Every employee within an organization is a potential problem, so the best approach is to view *all* employees with a healthy dose of skepticism.

Employees with different duties pose differing risks to trade secrets. To understand its overall exposure, your company has to look at its structure and segregate its employees into distinct groups. By evaluating the degree of access each group of employees has to trade secrets, your company will be better able to limit its exposure. Without attempting to propose sweeping generalizations, a brief analysis of selected employee groups is helpful to the person responsible for setting up a Trade Secret Protection Program for your corporation.

The Top Corporate Executive

It is a fact of life that top corporate executives have access to virtually any trade secret information a corporation possesses. Unless the executive is disgruntled or currently is being recruited by a competitor, the risk posed to trade secrets by the top executive is by unintentional disclosure, not direct theft. Then the problem is not so much access to trade secrets as it is constant contact and negligence. The executive may begin to take trade secrets for granted. The casual luncheon meeting, dinner with friends, the extemporaneous response to a press inquiry, and the executive-to-executive meetings are where the top executive is most likely to slip and unintentionally disclose trade secrets.

Clerical Personnel

Secretaries and other clerical personnel have great potential access to a broad range of corporate trade secrets. They handle, copy, and coordinate the dissemination of all corporate information, including trade secrets. Their omnipresent anonymity makes them a critical link in the trade secret chain that has to be closely watched if trade secrets are to remain safe. The indispensable role of secretaries and clerks in a corporation makes it common to forget the danger they present if they are not properly monitored. If anyone questions the importance of clerical personnel, just remember what happened in Watergate and how the documents were leaked.

High-Level Research Personnel

Employees who work with the high-level research and development divisions of a company are the most obvious problem areas for any corporation. Although just about anything is possible, they are the most prone to recruitment by competitors. When they leave, there is tremendous temptation to take with them the fruits of the research/ development activities of their former employers. Since limiting access to technical trade secrets is counterproductive with these employees, they must be continually educated and reminded about the key role of trade secrets to the corporation, how any disclosure could be extremely serious, and the certainty of a direct legal response against them personally if trade secrets are disclosed.

Technical and Engineering Support Personnel

Technical support staff develop an understanding of know-how and the practical side of technical corporate trade secret information. Although they usually do not have a comprehensive technical competence, technical staff represent a genuine danger point. A competitor will find them easy to attract because they can be hired for relatively modest salaries and take with them a great deal of practical information of immediate benefit to a competitor. By restricting the scope of technical trade secrets to which these employees will have access and advising them of the legal steps that will be taken against them, the likelihood of their leaving and disclosing secrets to a competitor may be contained somewhat.

Corporate Planning and Marketing Employees

Information relating to corporate marketing constitutes a valuable trade secret, particularly where principal competitors do not have a distinct technological advantage. Since the implementation of planning and marketing functions requires the involvement of large numbers of employees, there are multiple opportunities for the disclosure of trade secrets. Whether the disclosures are intentional or unintentional, a Comprehensive Trade Secret Program is essential to maintain secrecy until the appropriate moment. The Apple Computer Company's secrecy surrounding the introduction of its MacIntosh™ computer is a good example of how this is possible, even in a large company, in a very competitive industry. Apple wanted to test out

MacIntosh™ in a practical manner to work out the bugs prior to marketing this small personal computer. For more than one year prior to its introduction, suppliers and companies friendly to Apple, including its public accounting firm, used models in their offices. The secrecy umbrella placed around the testing was very effectively accomplished.

Financial and Operational Employees

Within every organization is the staff responsible for financing and handling ongoing operations. In order to function effectively, these employees have to work with numerous employees and many outsiders through the overall operation. This is an area of employee exposure to trade secrets that is frequently overlooked. The major risk here is the large quantity of people who are involved on a continuing basis. It is easy to become careless and not give proper attention to procedures relating to handling trade secrets. Constant employee educational efforts are required.

Custodial Staff

While the custodial employees are the lowest paid level in a corporation, they have free access to most corporate trade secrets. Besides being able to appear at almost any part of a company's operations without being questioned, many operate at night or on weekends when no one else is present. One high-tech company found out too late that a member of its custodial staff had rigged the office photocopying machine in such a manner as to produce a second copy of each document during office hours. The second copy remained unseen on the inside of the machine until it was picked up by the night custodian. Valuable trade secrets were passed on to a competitor before the employee was caught. A trade secret program must take into account access of custodial employees to trade secrets.

The Need for Pre-Employment Screening Procedures

Initially begin at the point before an employee is hired. A three-step pre-employment screening process is recommended for prospective employees.

Step One—What Role Will Trade Secrets Play in the Activities of a Potential Employee?

For every position, from custodian up to chief executive officer, there are certain activities or situations where an employee will have access to corporate trade secrets. As part of your company's formulation of a trade secret program, isolate the types of trade secrets to which a potential employee will have access and then categorize in absolute terms the value of those trade secrets to your corporation. The degree of exposure to trade secrets and their value to your corporation will dictate how carefully you should screen and hire potential applicants for the job. Before interviewing commences for a position involving major trade secret access, the person doing the hiring should have a single page summary of the corporate trade secret system and those secrets to which the position will be important.

Step Two—Evaluating the Prospective Employee.

Assuming you have a position to fill and the person to be hired will have access to valuable trade secrets, what techniques should be used in the evaluation process?

The Applicant's Résumé

An employer cannot assume an applicant's résumé is accurate. Résumé fraud is rampant. Recent studies conducted by employment experts have suggested that résumés submitted by job seekers contain false and misleading information more than 50 percent of the time. Employers must verify even basic facts such as an applicant's degrees and the claimed work experience in a particular industry. According to some experts, between 5 and 20 percent of résumés either intentionally distort or lie about educational degrees and job experience. The problem presented is the cost of verifying information. This is especially true in companies which hire many employees. There are companies which specialize in verifying résumé information. Since lying on a résumé may be symptomatic of dishonesty, where valuable trade secrets are involved with the job, any discrepancy on the résumé means you should look elsewhere.

References

Unfortunately, most résumés today do not contain names of specific references. Try to elicit multiple names and phone numbers. References should be verified after the interview is concluded, not before. You should seek verification, if at all possible, by contacting former associates who either worked for or under the direction of the applicant. Always go one level beyond what is offered. Checking in this manner opens up sources of information not available at the time of the interview.

Criminal/Military Record

Military and criminal records are relevant sources. It pays to verify the accuracy of the representations. While this is frequently done in connection with government-related projects, verification is no less important where commercial secrets are involved. If you are not able to verify the military record, ask for a copy of the discharge papers to be supplied after the interview. Make employment contingent on obtaining all relevant records.

Financial Standing

Consideration should be given to the salary level being offered and the existing financial standing and expectations of the job applicant. Beware of an applicant for a sensitive position whose life style or ambitions are not commensurate with the salary being offered. The high-roller usually means big problems. Include a credit check authorization waiver as part of the employment application where permissible. This will give you a great deal of valuable information.

Step Three—The Employment Interview and the Presentation of the Corporate Policy on Trade Secrets to Potential Employees

Throughout the employment interview probe for indications of trustworthiness. Even assuming technical competence for the position, the ability to keep trade secrets is a qualification that has to be independently evaluated. Search for attitudes toward former employers and how the candidate perceives his ethical responsibilities to those who employ him. Use hypothetical questions which will force the job applicant to choose between alternatives and analyze his responses. Ambiguity or ambivalence toward ethical situations are danger signals. Consider submitting candidates for high-level positions involving trade secrets to psychological screening tests. They can be helpful in getting an objective evaluation.

Part of the employment interview should be devoted to a detailed explanation of the employer's corporate policy on trade secrets and how it would directly affect the employee. Tell the potential employee about the types of corporate trade secrets to which he would be given access. It must be made lucidly clear that the employer feels very strongly about its trade secrets and will go to any length to protect them. As a precondition to employment, the employee must understand he will be required to execute a secrecy agreement which will clearly define his trade secret obligations to the employer. Since most employees do not have employment contracts, the secrecy agreement will often be an independent document.

This approach serves a three-fold purpose. First, a screening of the employee's attitudes toward trade secrets as well as normal job applications is possible before a hiring decision is made. Second, educating a potential employee from the earliest possible point will reinforce the Corporate Trade Secret Policy particularly if the program is more structured or formalized than those of previous employers. And third, the interview will serve as the basis from which the employee secrecy agreement will emerge. The employee will not be able to claim surprise at the explicit nature of the contract. The terms of the secrecy agreement should not be negotiable. The framework of the secrecy agreement and the interview should be viewed as an employee conditioning process. From the very beginning, the employee is forced to understand his employer has an aggressive policy to protect its trade secrets and all legal options will be exercised in the event trade secrets are wrongfully disclosed.

How to Deal with Employees and Trade Secrets During the Term of Employment

The Requirement of an Employee Secrecy Agreement

An employee who will have access to valuable trade secrets should be made to sign a contract obligating him to maintain the confidential nature of the trade secrets of employer. The agreement can be part of an employment contract, but since most employees do not have employment contracts, it should be a separate trade secret agreement. An example of an employee secrecy agreement is set forth below:

EMPLOYEE SECRECY AGREEMENT

I, _____, am an employee of
_____ Company. As part of my duties, I have access to trade secrets of my employer such as _____
_____. All knowledge and information I gain from those trade secrets and the trade secrets themselves, including all unpatented inventions, designs, know-how, trade secrets, technical information and data, specifications, blueprints, transparencies, test data and additions, modifications, and improvements thereon which are revealed to me shall for all time and for all purposes be regarded by me as strictly confidential and held in trust by me. I will not reveal or disclose the trade secrets to any other person, firm, corporation, company, or entity now or at any time in the future unless my employer instructs me to do so in writing. This secrecy protection will continue even if I no longer am employed by _____. I understand that if I reveal the trade secrets to unauthorized persons I personally may be subject to penalties and lawsuits for injunctive relief and money damages as well as possible criminal charges by my employer.

I acknowledge that I have read and understood the contents of this Agreement and freely sign it with the intent to be legally bound hereby.

WITNESS

_____

_____
(NAME)

_____
(PLACE SIGNED)

_____
(DATE)

From a legal standpoint, it is important that the secrecy agreement be signed *before* the employee starts to work. Courts are more likely to enforce a secrecy restriction if it is agreed that the employee would not have been hired unless he agreed to the secrecy provisions. An employee who is asked to sign a secrecy agreement after commencing employment may later assert he never voluntarily agreed to the restrictive conditions. Employees may claim these new terms of secrecy were forced upon them by the employer in order for them to keep their jobs. Courts look for "consideration" in contracts. That is, if an employee gets a job in exchange for agreeing to secrecy, this agreement is enforceable. However, if the employee gets the job and is performing it satisfactorily, a court might not then allow the employer (after hiring the person) to make secrecy a pre-condition of continuing employment. This is especially crucial if the employment contract or secrecy agreement contains binding secrecy obligations which will continue after the employee is no longer working for his employer.

The secrecy agreement should contain a description of the types of trade secrets to which the employee will have access. The employment agreement or secrecy agreement must also explain what happens when the employee either voluntarily leaves for a new job or has been discharged. The contract must prohibit the employee from disclosing trade secrets to a future employer or using them for his or her own benefit.

Another aspect of this area is the covenant not to compete. This is a contractual obligation prohibiting an employee from working for competitors in the future. There is no uniform rule of law in the United States on the extent to which an employer can realistically restrain former employees from competing after employment has terminated. It is necessary to examine the law of each individual state, because some legislatures have passed specific statutes on covenants not to compete. For example, California law provides that a contract preventing an employee from working for a competitor is in most cases unenforceable (Cal. Bus. Prof. Code §16600 (West, 1964)). Further, many state court decisions govern whether or not "covenants to compete" or contractual prohibitions on disclosing trade secret information will be enforceable after termination of employment. Courts are reluctant to enforce restrictive employee contracts even where they are not prohibited by law, so it is best for you not to overreach.

There are four elements courts generally look for in deciding if a former employee is to keep information a trade secret: the information in the possession of the former employee must be a genuine commercial trade secret; the former employer made every reasonable effort to keep the trade secret protected from disclosure; the former employee knew or should have known it was a trade secret; and the unauthorized use or appropriation of the trade secret by a former employee will do serious harm to the former employer. Judges look unfavorably on secrecy agreements which appear to prevent someone from using his skills to make a living. Someone who is a computer analyst by training and experience cannot be kept from performing activities for other employers, even if that person has previously signed a secrecy agreement including a covenant not to compete. Many courts will enforce provisions relating to non-competition issues if the geographic territory, scope of activities an employee can engage in, and the length of the non-compete provision are reasonable. It is also worth noting that a federal court in Michigan upheld an antitrust judgment based upon the use of a non-compete clause. This can be a sleeper, so be careful in contracts.

In summary, the less reasonable the restraints which exist in secrecy agreements, the less likely a court will be to enforce them.

Mandated Employee Educational Updates

Employees, regardless of length of service, must be continually updated on their obligation to protect corporate trade secrets. This is true for all employees—those with short and long years of service. While you should place primary emphasis on updating those employees who have access to the commercially critical trade secrets, all employees should be involved on a regular basis in the same way.

Every employer should schedule periodic seminars (at least annually) and educational updates with all employees. During the educational sessions, employees should receive a review of the overall corporate trade secret policy, with emphasis given to those procedures in place. The employer should solicit the employees' suggestions as to how the trade secret program is, or should be, handled. Employee suggestions improve the overall program by directly involving employees in the planning process.

Employees have to appreciate that protection and non-disclosure of trade secrets are primary conditions of their employment. One company has required its employees to execute a written acknowledgement, every two years, of the secrecy obligations which they signed when initially hired. Although such acknowledgment in itself has no great legal significance, the ritual of the affirmation is likely to reinforce an employee's understanding of the employer's policy on trade secrets.

How to React to the Employee Suspected of Stealing Trade Secrets

When you suspect an employee of stealing trade secrets, should he be fired immediately or is a more conservative approach advisable? When a corporation's most critical corporate trade secrets are involved, an employer has no option but to act immediately.

A sophisticated corporate trade secret enforcement policy has its enforcement options outlined and established in advance of any problem. The first line of defense is to seek a court injunction to prohibit the employee from further wrongful disclosures. Injunctions are not automatic and documentation is crucial. A court will not issue an injunction unless a company can show it has or will suffer "irreparable harm" as a result of an employee's actions. The existence of a signed secrecy agreement or an employment contract with specific secrecy covenants binding the employee is most helpful to a lawyer asking the court to grant an injunction. Where the employee has not signed any secrecy document, the court must be persuaded by evidence that the employee is violating a confidence. Proving the secrecy duty without some written document is more difficult. The top research employee within an organization, because of his position, will be presumed to have a higher duty to maintain corporate secrets. On the other hand, the low-paid non-professional employee who has no contract stands a better chance of avoiding an injunction. Although one's level of compensation is not the only criterion for determining responsibility to keep trade secrets, it is a factor courts often consider in their opinions. Of course, an employer can seek money damages for damage to trade secrets as part of the injunction process, but major attention must remain with stopping theft with a court injunction.

The employer's second option against the thieving employee is the initiation of a criminal action. The specific laws of each state as well as federal statutes should be consulted to determine if it is a realistic possibility in a particular case. For example, in 1983 in a California federal court, criminal indictments resulted from cooperation between the United States Justice Department and a major United States computer manufacturer that wanted to stop theft of its most sensitive trade secrets. The indictments were handed down against some of its employees and those of a competitor who was allegedly trying to bribe employees to obtain trade secrets. This shows that state and federal criminal statutes can be an effective weapon if properly used in an appropriate situation. The existence of such criminal sanctions, particularly if clearly communicated to employees, is an effective deterrent to trade secret theft.

You must recognize that the employee with an employment contract for a set term is difficult to discharge without "cause." Mere suspicion that the employee is stealing or misappropriating trade secrets is not sufficient cause. Discharge of an employee for stealing trade secrets, if not properly documented, may result in lawsuits by the former employee for wrongful termination of employment or for alleged damage to his reputation resulting from unsubstantiated libel or slander by the former employer. It is legally possible for an employee to force an employer to reinstate him and to pay damages at the same time. Therefore, the employer has to make every effort to document the employee's wrongful acts.

If an employee is stealing secrets, the major area of concern should be who is the ultimate beneficiary? It is critical to know how stolen or misappropriated trade secrets will be used. Where your employee intends to go into competition, an immediate legal response is most often advisable unless there are countervailing antitrust aspects. Where the trade secrets are being passed on to a competitor or other third party, identification of the end user ought to take a higher priority than an immediate legal reaction against the employer. The premature firing of an employee before the end user of the trade secrets is discovered may simply result in another employee taking the place of the first.

In short, employers must convince their employees that a swift, unavoidable response will occur if there is any theft or misappropriation of trade secrets. The employee must know with certainty that he risks civil and potential criminal litigation as well as loss of his job when he misuses trade secrets.

How to React when Your Employee Announces He Is Leaving

When a long-term or valuable employee announces his intention to leave, will the trade secrets now in his head end up in the hands of a competitor? Assuming your employee has executed an enforceable secrecy agreement, there are other steps you can take to minimize the risk your trade secrets are not misused. While there is no single best approach, what follows are good techniques.

The Employee Exit Interview

When an employee voluntarily decides to terminate his employment, an employer hopefully receives at least some minimal advance notice. Immediately schedule a detailed employee exit interview. During the interview ask the employee to disclose frankly the reasons for the voluntary termination and where he intends to go. Although an employee cannot be forced to reveal this information, a firm inquiry frequently yields at least some information that is helpful. From a practical standpoint if your employee has accumulated sick benefits, vacation days, or other outstanding benefits, it is unlikely he will be totally uncooperative if he expects to receive the benefits in a timely manner.

Whether or not an employee admits that he intends to work for a competitor, the exit interview is the final opportunity to reeducate the employee on his contractual obligations concerning trade secrets that should continue even after he leaves. When the employee has signed an employment contract with secrecy provisions or an individual secrecy agreement, the document should be examined with the employee point-by-point. Avoid conducting the exit interview as a hostile confrontation. Its purpose is to remind the employee of his legal obligations so that in subsequent employment activities he is not in violation of any legal obligations. Nevertheless, try to leave the strong impression that immediate legal action will occur in the event the employee subsequently discloses trade secrets without your prior written authorization.

You should develop in advance a standard checklist of the points to cover at all exit interviews. Items such as the terms of the employment contract or the secrecy agreement, the legal obligation to return all copies of corporate documents and items to the employer, and possible legal actions in the event trade secret restrictions are violated should be included. Some companies list these items on a document and the employee is asked to acknowledge that the points have been covered with him at the conclusion of the interview. Unless the exit interview situation is conducted in a highly hostile atmosphere, employees are often willing to sign a written acknowledgment of their continuing trade secret obligations. The existence of a signed affirmation is useful in court if it is later necessary to show that a former employee understood his trade secret contractual liabilities prior to leaving his job. In fact, where a former employee gives oral testimony that totally contradicts the secrecy documents, a trial attorney can use a written acknowledgement to impeach the credibility and truthfulness of the former employee in court.

When an exit interview is not possible, send a certified letter to the employee's last known address confirming the following points: the existence of the employee's signed secrecy agreement; an outline of the corporate policy on trade secrets; a demand for the return of all trade secret documents and copies in the former employee's possession; and a description of the legal options available to the employer if trade secrets are later revealed without authorization. The letter should ask the former employee to sign and return it as an acknowledgment. While a refusal by a former employee to sign an acknowledgment is not proof of anything, you still might be able to explain to a court how you made every reasonable effort to protect yourself from the unauthorized actions of a former employee.

The Post-Employment Consultation Relationship

For the top employees who intend to leave, consider offering them the opportunity to act as paid consultants after employment terminates. Although this option means a direct expenditure, there are at least two important benefits. First, if the employee enters into a contractual consulting relationship with you, it is legally permissible to place new conditions regarding trade secrets upon a former employee. The consulting position makes the additional restrictions legally enforceable. Second, by continuing to receive some compensation, the former employee is less likely to use trade secrets to the detriment of a former employer.

Some lawyers advise their clients to have former employees sign a continuing secrecy agreement at the time they are terminated. Some employers insist that such a document be signed before final vacation days or other accrued benefits are paid. The problem with this approach is that it may not be legally enforceable. Courts tend to strike down such contracts as either unreasonable or unfairly forced upon the employee since the employee had already earned the benefits that were threatened to be withheld. This is why retaining key employees as paid consultants after employment terminates makes more sense.

Periodic Employment Update Checks

Former employees who had access to valuable trade secrets are under no obligation to advise their former employers of current employment status. Tracking the activities of such high-risk individuals is valuable for a period of time. At the time of termination, employees having access to top trade secrets and presenting the greatest risk should be identified. At least on a semi-annual basis, consider instituting informal checks to find out where and for whom they are working.

In most cases, this is a simple task and can be quickly accomplished by in-house staff without the need to hire outside investigators.

In conducting update checks, employers should pay particular attention to former employees who have started their own businesses. Technological overlaps, if any, existing between the products or services supplied by the former employee's new company and your operations could be a sign of trouble.

Conclusion

Access makes the employee the most significant risk to trade secrets. By establishing and following specifically designed procedures for handling employees prior to, during, and after employment, it is possible to minimize the exposure of your trade secrets.

5

Binding the Non-Employee to Protect Your Trade Secrets

Every company has to share its trade secrets with outsiders at some point. It is critical to bind consultants, agents, bankers, and subcontractors so that they maintain the confidentiality of your trade secrets. This chapter presents specific procedures for controlling outsiders as well as handling unsolicited submissions of trade secrets.

How the Outsiders You Deal with Are a
Threat to Your Trade Secrets

No company or business organization can operate in a vacuum. Skills and resources from outside an organization are frequently needed. When trade secrets have to be disclosed to outside parties, the trade secret owner must take great care to adequately protect trade secrets while in the hands of authorized outsiders. An error can be fatal to trade secrets. Disclosure, when made in a proper manner, can effectively protect the confidential nature of trade secrets and limit their use. This chapter presents methods for disclosure of trade secrets to outsiders and points out the problems different types of outsiders might present.

Our courts come down very hard on trade secret owners who allow outsiders unrestricted access to trade secrets.

Outside parties do *not* have any formal obligation to protect your trade secrets, unless you tell them the information is a trade secret and that they may not reveal them to anyone without your permission. Advise outsiders that the information is a trade secret before or at the time of the disclosure. In some cases, the courts have ruled that the trade secrets were no longer secret and were free to anyone. Obviously, do not disclose trade secrets to any outsider unless workable procedures for protecting them while in his possession are already in place.

Documents containing trade secrets on their face should be clearly marked as follows:

<u>N-O-T-I-C-E</u>

TRADE SECRET OF _____ COMPANY—DO NOT DISCLOSE TO ANYONE WITHOUT PRIOR WRITTEN PERMISSION OF _____

Or

PROPRIETARY INFORMATION/TRADE SECRET—DISCLOSURE PROHIBITED UNDER PENALTY OF LAW

Or

NOTICE—THIS DOCUMENT CONTAINS TRADE SECRET INFOR-MATION OF _____COMPANY. UN-AUTHORIZED DISCLOSURE WILL RESULT IN CRIMINAL AND/OR CIVIL LIABILITY TO YOU.

Or

WARNING: TRADE SECRET DOCUMENT. DISCLOSURE WILL RESULT IN SERIOUS LEGAL PROBLEMS FOR YOU. DO NOT COPY OR SHOW TO ANYONE WITHOUT PERMISSION.

Oral notification is not adequate to protect your trade secrets. For example, assume you show a trade secret document to a consultant working for your company. The consultant then, without authorization, passes on the document to another company. Your failure to place a written notice trade secret legend on the document may mean the other company is unaware of the document's trade secret status. While your consultant is legally at fault, the outside company may not be liable and may be free to use your trade secrets if it doesn't know of the unauthorized action of the consultant.

Unfortunately, outsiders who are given access to your trade secrets rarely appreciate the sensitive nature of the information they receive. What is a trade secret in one business may be common knowledge in another. Outsiders will unknowingly reveal information, unless they are educated to appreciate the value of the trade secrets of your company. For example, the conclusions and data from a management consulting company's market research conducted for your company on a specific product's salability in a geographic area can be useful to a competitor. When your outside consultant finishes a research project, you should send a letter to the consultant specifying that the work performed and the data and conclusions are not to be made available to any other party. Do this even if the initial contract with the firm specified non-disclosure. Obviously, a contract and written reminder will not prevent an unscrupulous consultant from unauthorized use of the information, but it places the owner of the trade secrets in a firm legal position if a court is subsequently asked to enforce the secrecy agreement or to award damages. A forceful, dynamic approach is the goal.

You must always assume that outsiders with access to your company's trade secrets are tempted to use the information to advance their business interests or for personal profit. The risks vary according to the type of outsider and trade secrets involved. Intentional misappropriation by lawyers or certified public accountants is unlikely because of their Codes of Professional Responsibility requiring strict confidentiality and ethical rules. Greater potential risks are business consultants, financial institutions, outside suppliers, and subcontractors who each have multiple reasons to be interested in your trade secrets. Where your trade secrets are involved, the business reputation of a party becomes as important in the selection of an outsider as do specific skills to perform a trade.

The Importance of Requiring a Third-Party Secrecy Agreement

Before revealing any trade secrets to outsiders, decide whether a secrecy agreement should be signed by the outsider. Without any question, a secrecy agreement is a precondition to disclosure when trade secrets of genuine commercial value are involved.

There is an important legal reason for requiring secrecy agreements. A properly drafted, signed agreement constitutes a specific legal obligation. Think of a trade secret agreement signed by an outsider as the beginning of a trial. Trade secrets are traced from your company to the outsider by examining the legal chain of custody. The point is—never break the chain. If any question arises at a later point, the existence of a signed agreement by the outsider shows he was put on notice about your trade secrets and you took every reasonable effort to protect their confidentiality. The contract is the crucial link in the chain. In a court of law, the existence of the signed agreement constitutes "prima facie evidence" of notice and the trade secret status of the corporate documents. Particularly when you are seeking a court injunction, the written secrecy agreement outlining trade secret obligations is an essential piece of evidence needed to obtain approval of the court.

Who Should Sign Secrecy Agreements

Having a corporation execute a secrecy agreement on its behalf and for its employees may not be enough. Give serious consideration in each case as to whether individual employees of the outsider must sign individual employee secrecy agreements binding them formally. To decide if this procedure makes sense, take a close look at the structure, size, and quality of the organization to which your trade secrets may be revealed. Where the outsider is a small corporation owned and controlled by a single individual, requiring the owner personally to execute a secrecy agreement is a worthwhile safeguard. Such a contract can be the basis for holding the individual personally liable in the event there is an unauthorized leak of your trade secrets.

From a strategy standpoint, the legal enforceability of the agreement should be a less important consideration than the ability to impress upon that individual the importance of protecting your trade secrets. The degree of trade secret disclosure is an element in the individual secrecy contract evolution. Where the trade secrets are relatively unimportant, requiring individual secrecy agreements once the employer has signed is not a top priority. However, when trade secrets have great commercial value for the trade secret holder, individual secrecy agreements ought to be a prerequisite to disclosure.

Your company must determine which employees of the outsider company represent the greatest potential risk to your trade secrets. The relationship of those key employees to their employer is very relevant. A person who is a long-term employee or has an ownership interest in a company is not as likely to abuse the responsibility surrounding trade secrets as are others. Obviously, this type of employee has much more to lose in the event of a problem. On the other hand, for the employee with a brief tenure and a history of frequently changing employers an individual secrecy agreement is an absolute prerequisite to disclosure.

Pay close attention when trade secrets are disclosed to a subsidiary, a division, or related entity of a larger corporate structure. The secrecy agreement must define the extent of the disclosure permitted within the company and address the issue of whether a subsidiary is permitted to reveal your trade secrets to a parent corporation. Key questions to ask—Are there restrictions on the disclosure? Will a parent corporation or related corporations be permitted access at their own request to trade secret information held by another? What happens if a company with access to your trade secrets is acquired by your competitor? The responses to these questions in some circumstances suggest that secrecy agreements for individual employees are advisable as well as secrecy agreements with parent corporations, subsidiaries, and related companies.

Eight Key Points to Include in an Outsider Trade Secret Agreement

No single secrecy agreement can cover all possible situations. However, since the extent and the reasons for trade secret disclosures vary in each case, tailor the provisions of your secrecy agreements to meet each particular circumstance. Consult an experienced attorney to assist to develop a standardized format for your company. To help in analyzing your company's particular needs, review the following eight basic points.

Point One—The Designation of Trade Secrets

Include in your secrecy agreements with outsiders an appendix describing in detail exactly what type of trade secret information is given. A general reference to "all trade secret information to chemical processes" is inadequate. A description of trade secrets demands specificity. Where it is reasonable, the appendix should describe individual documents by name, length, and general content. If a particular document is lengthy, a narrative description of the document should be included as part of the appendix. Clearly listing the trade secret information will permit your legal counsel to prove, if necessary, to a court that the outsider understood a particular document is proprietary, that you viewed it as a trade secret, and that it was not to be disclosed. The secrecy agreement will confirm that all documents containing trade secrets are marked with a clear and unambiguous legend. One approach is to number consecutively pages of all documents revealed to an outsider so that when a project is completed, you can be sure a complete set of all documents will be returned.

Point Two—The Scope of the Disclosure

A secrecy agreement must clearly state the purpose for the disclosure. The purpose of the disclosure is directly tied to the "scope" of the secrets that are provided to an outsider. For example, where raw manufacturing data is given to a consulting engineeer so that he may make a comparison with other competitive companies, the scope of the disclosure is for the *limited* purpose of the comparative analysis. Or, if your subcontractor is given trade secrets necessary to manufacture a particular subcomponent for you, a secrecy agreement with the subcontractor must limit disclosure and application of trade secrets to that use only. You should specifically prohibit your subcontractor by contract from using the secrets for his individual benefit or sharing them in any manner without your prior written permission. If the outsider is later found to have used or disclosed the trade secrets in an unauthorized manner, a written prohibition in the contract will help your lawyer to prove that the wrongful disclosure by the sub-contractor was willful and not an oversight. Demonstrating intentional disclosure of your secrets by the subcontractor gives you a better chance to get injunctive relief and punitive damages. Therefore, the clear definition of the "scope" of disclosure is very important.

Point Three—The Duration of Disclosure

Stipulate in your secrecy agreement a specific duration for the trade secret disclosure. When the time has expired, there must be an affirmative legal responsibility to return to you the trade secrets and to destroy all copies. For example, if a subcontractor is provided with certain trade secrets in order to assist him in manufacturing a device, stipulate that the secrecy agreement requires the trade secrets to be used only as long as the subcontractor manufactures the device to your satisfaction. When production stops or your relationship terminates, the subcontractor must immediately return the trade secrets and cease all activities involved with them. It must be indisputably clear that the subcontractor has no independent rights to the trade secret information. A time period, even if artificially derived, is helpful in periodically evaluating when trade secrets ought to be returned.

Point Four—The Affirmative Obligations of the Outsider to You

Most individuals and companies react most responsibly when they have a recognized set of rules or procedures to follow. To guarantee maximum cooperation, outline in detail the responsibilities of the outsider in using your trade secrets, which it is required to observe at all times. For example, require in your secrecy agreement that all trade secret documents and materials, including all copies or physical reproductions, be returned at the conclusion of the assignment for which the outsider was hired. If you permit the outsider to make copies of documents, require the outsider to keep permanent records of how many copies are made and to designate which specific employees have possession of the secret documents. Insist on a contact person who is an employee of the outsider and who is responsible for tracking the location of documents at all times. Stay in contact with that person on a continuing basis. An independent audit is one way to periodically monitor whether trade secrets are being properly handled by the outsider. This, however, would have to be part of the secrecy agreement or other contract.

If your trade secret documents or the information they contain are inputted into a computer data bank or word processing storage system, you may want the right to know at all times: in what form it is stored; how accessible it is; and which outsider employees will work with the trade secrets on an ongoing basis. Obviously, tracking information, once it is committed to electronic storage, is difficult. Nevertheless, make every reasonable effort to follow the trail in order to protect the trade secrets status.

Other examples of responsibilities you may wish to include in a secrecy agreement are: the segregation of trade secrets; procedures for selecting employees who will have access to the trade secrets; physical security procedures; notice when unauthorized disclosure occurs; and restrictions on disclosure to unrelated parties.

Point Five—Requiring Individual Secrecy Agreements from Employees of Outsiders

In your secrecy agreement specify whether individual secrecy agreements of outsider employees are required as a precondition to trade secret disclosure. The best approach is always to keep your options open. Reserve the right to demand at any time that employees of an outsider sign individual secrecy agreements.

It is not unusual for a company to have had its employees bound internally by its own form of secrecy agreements. You will find these outsiders will normally object to a requirement that their employees sign a second secrecy agreement. They will argue that their employees are already covered by a secrecy agreement. If confronted with this argument, take a moment to review their standard employee secrecy agreement. Evaluate if it is satisfactory for your purposes. It may or may not be. At the same time verify which employees have actually signed the employer's standard agreement. Not infrequently, you will discover internal secrecy agreements are signed by some but not all employees. As a general rule, insist your secrecy agreement be signed at least by key employees who will use your trade secrets regardless of the other agreements they have signed for their employer. Again, the individual secrecy agreements give you a right to go after the individual employee, not just the employer. This is why it is important. Be very firm in negotiating this point.

Point Six—Require that All Necessary Parties Execute the Secrecy Agreement

When trade secrets are revealed to a division or subsidiary of a company, have the agreement signed by the appropriate corporate officials. Check with your lawyer as to how you should bind the division of a larger company. It may be necessary in some cases for the corporate officers of the parent or holding company to sign their own individual confidentiality and secrecy agreements. Tactically, attempt to have the highest level of official with the outsider company sign the agreement. It is vital to impress upon top-level management the seriousness of the trade secret disclosure and the degree of corporate exposure if there is a misuse of those secrets.

Point Seven—The Role of Liquidated Damages

Consider if you want your secrecy agreement to include a section on liquidated damages. Liquidated damages is a legal device in a contract which establishes in advance the monetary value of your loss in the event trade secrets are disclosed without authorization. From a legal standpoint, liquidated damages will not be enforced by a court, unless they bear a realistic relationship to the anticipated damages that could result if the worst happens. A court makes its determination of reasonableness based on the types of secrets involved and their relative value. For example, if a document contained a key corporate strategy (a trade secret) and it was leaked to a competitor by the employee of a consultant working for your company, you would have the basis for legal action against the consultant and its employee for violation of the secrecy obligation. If the employee's individual secrecy agreement contained a liquidated damage clause providing he would be personally liable for $100,000 in damages, a court might be convinced that the $100,000 liquidated damage provision was enforceable. The main point of liquidated damages is to frighten away those who might be tempted to misuse trade secrets. Because liquidated damages are an actual determined amount, this is in many cases a more real deterrent than simply saying "someday you will have a court decide what damages you owe." Liquidated damages tend to temper avarice in a way the mere threat of a lawsuit does not. Where you insert liquidated damages in a secrecy agreement, do not make them so high as to be unjustifiable. This is not to suggest, though, that a liquidated damages provision with a large dollar value isn't enforceable. High liquidated damage clauses serve as a clear warning as to the importance of trade secrets to your company.

Point Eight—The Term of the Secrecy Agreement

The secrecy agreement must require an outsider and its employees to keep your trade secret information confidential even after a formal working relationship has ended. For example, if a management consultant receives trade secrets in order to conduct market research, the completion of the project after six months and the return of documents to you in no way voids the consultant's continuing obligation to keep the information secret. To avoid any misunderstandings, the secrecy agreement should bind outsiders for a specific period of time. Since public policy favors the disclosure of information, most courts closely scrutinize contracts which say "ABC Company will keep the trade secrets of XYZ Company secret forever." Where the parties to an agreement have negotiated a time period which is arguably reasonable, courts are more likely to enforce it.

Techniques for Dealing with Specific Types of Outsiders

It is always an awkward situation when asking an outsider to sign a secrecy agreement. "Don't you trust me?" or "I have never had anyone ask for one before, I've never signed one, and I don't intend to start now" are common responses. Different approaches are needed for "smoothing ruffled feathers" and dealing with varying types of outsiders.

The Dilemma of Dealing with Corporate Officers and Directors of an Outsider Company

Regardless of the scope of the activities an outsider is doing for your company or the outsider's size, top officers and directors of the outsider can obtain access to your trade secrets if they desire. In all likelihood, they will refuse to sign any type of individual secrecy agreement. While they probably will freely impose the requirement on lower-level employees who will work directly with the trade secrets, they will balk at signing themselves. Make the judgment of whether or not to disclose in the face of such refusals. In all likelihood, you will decide to disclose anyway. If this is the case, in all contacts with these individuals in their privileged positions, stress the importance of following your trade secrets within their companies. Such educational "pep rallies" are helpful.

How to Approach Your Subcontractors

Subcontractors who will manufacture or produce products under contract with your company should, in every case, execute secrecy agreements where your trade secrets are used. Even after secrecy agreements are signed, the best technique is to reveal only what is required and not to expand the scope of disclosure unless specifically asked by the subcontractor. Where any question exists about the subcontractor's internal procedures for handling your trade secrets, ask for meetings with the specific in-house employees of your subcontractor who will work with your trade secrets. Evaluate the internal trade secret protection procedures of your subcontractor on a continuing basis to guarantee compliance. A visit several times a year for this purpose in most cases is sufficient. An annual reminder letter of what you expect is advisable.

Trade Secrets and Your Suppliers

Suppliers are normally not a major risk to trade secrets. A trade secret agreement is not necessary when suppliers only have limited access to trade secret information. Potential problems can arise when a supplier is providing a unique item which in itself may be valuable to others. For example, if your company were producing a particular chemical formulation and the mix required an exotic chemical, the specific chemical and the quantity supplied to you by the outsider company could be valuable trade information to your competitor. In that case, you might require your supplier to sign a secrecy agreement prohibiting disclosure to any outside parties of the products and the quantities of those products it sells to your company.

The Role of Bankers and Financial Institutions

Typically, bankers and financial institutions want to know everything about a company when arranging financing. Although their major concern is adequate collateral for loans, their thirst for information can be unquenchable. However, bankers are not always attuned to the importance of trade secrets and the need to guard them against disclosure. Although banks are bound by ethical and legal constraints as to customer information, the dangers of disclosure, particularly casual disclosure, nevertheless exist. Ask your banker to sign a secrecy agreement and closely question the banker if he refuses.

The Venture Capital Lender

Particularly in high-tech ventures, much of the equity capital invested in new companies in recent years has come from venture capitalists. If the venture capitalist actually becomes an equity participant in your enterprise, there is little chance your trade secrets will be wrongfully or negligently disclosed. The potential risk arises when a number of venture capital firms are simultaneously reviewing your corporate information to decide if they desire to invest. The problem is a venture capitalist may be talking to you today and to your competition tomorrow. It is strongly recommended that you refuse to disclose without a secrecy agreement. You should not meet with too much opposition to this request from the better venture capitalists. They will probably accept and agree with your concerns about the need for strict procedures toward controlling trade secrets. In fact, this concern can make you look like a better candidate for favorable consideration.

What to Do with Agents and Sales Representatives

Depending on the activities in which they are involved, agents and sales representatives may require knowledge of your trade secrets to market your products effectively. Routinely ask them to sign trade secrecy agreements. What is more important is to provide continuing education programs along with periodic written reminders. With time, these will strongly demonstrate to them how you value your trade secrets and the need to be circumspect in their sales and promotional activities.

Your Accountants and Auditors

Outside accountants and auditors are not normally a trade secret problem. Since their function is primarily financial, the information they gather is not in itself of high value to a competitor. Even when an audit is being conducted, trade secrets play a minimal part. Therefore, insist on secrecy agreements only in an exceptional situation where trade secrets will be directly involved and you anticipate some risk or potential for conflict of interest.

An Area for Concern—Independent Consultants

Consultants ought to be a major concern. Consultants make a living by having multiple clients retain their services. The self-imposed ethical constraints of accountants and lawyers are not universally accepted by consultants. "Proper conduct" varies from firm to firm. Without exception, each independent consultant should agree to execute individually a secrecy agreement before being hired. At the end of each project remind the consultant in writing of its ongoing legal secrecy obligations, and place the consultant on notice that any unauthorized disclosure will result in immediate legal action against the company and employees individually. Surprisingly, outside consultants are rarely asked to sign secrecy agreements. Do not allow this mistake to happen in your company.

Talking with Potential Licensing or Joint Venture Partners

To locate the right partners and to consummate a licensing agreement or joint venture, critical trade secrets have to be disclosed to see if the overall deal makes sense. Without exception, have all potential partners and any other related parties sign secrecy agreements *before* entering into substantive negotiations where trade secrets will be made available as part of the negotiation process.

How to Handle the Request of an Outsider to Submit Trade Secrets to Your Company

Court decisions are replete with stories of those con men who make a living from fraudulently submitting ideas to companies and later filing lawsuits for alleging their ideas were stolen or appropriated without compensation. Your company must be prepared to respond when it receives an unsolicited letter or proposal from an unrelated company or person requesting your company to examine an invention or idea for possible acquisition. The entire area of unsolicited materials is fraught with potential pitfalls. There are some companies which adamantly refuse to accept anything from outside sources. They seem to share the attitude of either "if not invented here, it doesn't exist" or "self-protection is more important than seeking outside ideas.'' At the other end of the spectrum, there are companies which will agree to talk to anyone and evaluate a proposed idea. Neither attitude is a satisfactory approach to the problem. While it is counterproductive for a company to believe it can never benefit from outside input, it is reasonable and necessary to take all reasonable precautions when dealing with the outsiders.

If your company doesn't already have one, develop a formalized policy to deal with unsolicited submissions from outsiders. The basic format for a program is described below. First, under no circumstance should any employee review any idea, information, or documents at the time of its submission. All requests that are received should be directed to a single designated employee. Prepare a form letter in advance to be sent to any submitter of unsolicited information. The form letter clearly explains your corporate policy not to review any request, unless the submitter understands and agrees in writing to the terms of the corporate policy. The outsider must acknowledge that by accepting an idea for review your company is not creating a confidential relationship with the submitter. It must be totally within the discretion of your company to decide whether you will initiate discussions after examining the submission. The trick is not to write a letter that is so legalistic and one-sided that it is unintelligible and scares good prospects away. Remember, without a signed acknowledgment, return all submissions immediately.

If an acknowledgment is signed and you examine the submission, you may find you already have the same information within your business files. For this reason, exceptionally careful records must be kept from the time an inquiry is received through its final disposition. In the event of litigation, your company must demonstrate two points to defend itself successfully: first, evidence of an established corporate procedure for handling trade secrets and complete internal records showing the submitted information was handled in accordance with your procedures; second, that your company already knew about the invention or submitted information, the extent of corporate information at that time and that you immediately advised the outsider in writing.

Why You Must Be Cautious when Submitting
Documents to the United States Government

Increasingly, companies are required to submit all kinds of information to United States government officials, bureaus, and independent agencies. Do not overlook the existence of the "Freedom of Information Act." The Freedom of Information Act (FOI) makes any disclosure to the federal government or its agencies available to competitors or anyone else who makes an appropriate FOI request. Unless you specifically claim an eligible exception at the time of disclosure, as provided in the Freedom of Information Act, assume your information is available for the asking. Do not rely on an oral promise or understanding with a federal government employee or official. Even a general letter from the agency or office involved will not guarantee your proprietary information is immune from Freedom of Information Act requests from your competitors. When you provide the documents, send a letter outlining the confidential nature of documents you are disclosing and claim an exemption. It is possible your letter will become separated from the documents themselves. If this happens, a disclosure by the government may occur even if not authorized. Therefore, where appropriate, stamp each page of confidential documents with a trade secret FOI legend. One example is:

N-O-T-I-C-E

THIS DOCUMENT CONTAINS CONFIDENTIAL TRADE SECRET INFORMATION OF __(insert name)__. PURSUANT TO EXEMPTION B(4) OF THE FREEDOM OF INFORMATION ACT (5 U.S.C.A 552), THIS DOCUMENT AND ITS CONTENTS CANNOT BE REVEALED BY THE U.S. GOVERNMENT IN RESPONSE TO A FOI REQUEST.

Conclusion

Careful planning combined with very selective disclosures of trade secrets goes a long way toward preventing unauthorized trade secret disclosure by outsiders with whom your company works. In almost every instance, as a prerequisite to disclosure, demand the execution of a secrecy agreement by third parties.

6

Protecting Trade Secrets and Licensing of Technology

Licensing of trade secrets is complex and potentially profitable. This chapter provides an extensive analysis of the five stages of a licensing transaction. Practical suggestions are given on how to get the maximum benefit as a licensor of trade secrets while avoiding the very real risks.

What it Means to License Technology and Trade Secrets

A license agreement is a contract between two or more parties in which one party (the "licensor") transfers rights in its technology or trade secrets to another party ("the licensee"). Licenses of technology can be either exclusive or non-exclusive and may be limited to specified geographic territories and uses. Sometimes, two parties license technology to each other; this is called a "cross-license."

What kind of technology can be licensed? The answer is just about anything. When most executives hear about licensing they tend to think of a "patent" license, because historically companies transferred technology by licensing their patents or specific products and industrial processes. One license arrangement that underwent extensive antitrust scrutiny was the license to Mitsubishi Electric of Japan of patents on electrical power generating equipment of Westinghouse Electric Corporation.

Licensing of technology has undergone a major transition. Today, trade secrets are playing the predominant role in the transfer of technology. Even if a patent comprises a significant component of a license, trade secrets and know-how which are not publicly available tend to make up the critical value of a license.

This chapter will assume your company (as licensor) wants to license technology comprised of trade secret information for the purpose of entering a new market. The risk of improper disclosure could cause your valuable trade secrets to be irrevocably lost. We will review both the pitfalls and advantages of licensing. Then the five key stages of licensing trade secrets will be analyzed from the standpoint of the licensor.

Licensing Trade Secrets—The Advantages

There are at least four benefits that can come from licensing trade secrets. With the high cost and fluctuating availability of capital, trade secret licensing is a quick method for a company possessing trade secrets to benefit from entering a new market without the necessity of expending additional capital. By licensing, a company's financial risks can be limited to the possibility of not receiving royalties from the licensee because the licensee's use and products are not commercially successful in its market.

The limited commercial life of technical applications of some technologies almost requires licensing. A license of technology with prospects of quick return can be quite attractive as opposed to betting on long-term consumer demand. The rise and fall of consumer buying of home video games during 1981-1983 is a perfect example. Initially, there was great interest and massive consumer demand for new video games, particularly for use in the home television market. Unfortunately, by the time the 25 major (many new) companies competing to sell hardware and game cartridges geared up to the demand by late 1982, consumer interest in bouncing balls, gorillas that climb ladders and Pac-Man™ was on the wane. The crushing losses sustained by most companies in 1983 was based on one simple fact—the public became bored.

High-tech companies specializing in basic or applied technological innovation may be better off selling their technology through licenses and depending totally on continuing research efforts to produce leading-edge innovations for subsequent sale or licensing.

Another benefit of licensing is the relationship it creates. Licensing offers the possibility of learning more about another company. Through the negotiation process and the subsequent relationship of licensor and licensee, your company has the chance to evaluate the desirability of a long-term relationship with other companies. This is important because of the growing role of joint ventures as a way of doing business.

The opportunity for two companies to cross-license technologies is a distinct advantage. It is possible to improve a similar product line by combining joint efforts or expand horizons without creating a direct competitor through cross-licensing. In either case, with little or no additional research costs, significant strides can be made toward full technology utilization by a cross-license.

Finally, it is worth stating that some companies are better at marketing than innovation. Investors can profit more quickly from royalties from a well-marketed technology than from uneven returns from a mishandled in-house marketing effort.

Licensing Trade Secrets—The Disadvantages

The licensing of trade secrets can result in the creation of a serious competitor where none existed before. Since most trade secret licenses are to companies in similar lines of business, even licenses of seemingly unrelated technology can create very real, long-term competition for the licensor.

Many United States businesses do not look far enough into the future in their strategic corporate planning. For incentive-compensated executives, quarterly or annual profit projections take precedence over other planning considerations. Before contemplating a license of trade secrets, your company must take a realistic look at its strengths and weaknesses. Companies possessing a strong technological edge may lack production capacity, a distribution network, and the capital base essential to sustain aggressive marketing of products. Licensing is a logical alternative for those companies. However, short-term logic can sometimes overshadow the long-term dangers of licensing. With increased emphasis on technological leads, a license can give a presently dormant competitor the technological edge it needs to crush the licensor in head-to-head competition. Therefore, it is advisable to make the short-term profitability of a license transaction the *last* factor to be evaluated in studying whether or not it is worthwhile.

Consider the following points—what is the value of the trade secrets to your current operations, how could those trade secrets give your potential competitors a greater edge, and what is the realistic commercial life of your trade secrets? Only by keeping the answers to those questions in mind can you decide practically if the price offered by a prospective licensee for your trade secrets is enough. The possibility of creating a competitor by licensing has led many companies to seek out joint venture or acquisition activities instead. The joint venture/trade secret scenario, which sometimes presents greater control over trade secrets, is discussed in the following chapter.

Once the license is signed and the royalty timely paid, no need for further contact between the licensing partners exists, unless the license requires future transfers of information. This means your company as licensor will have increasing difficulty in tracking down what your licensee is doing with your trade secrets. This chapter will examine how you protect yourself against a licensee selling your trade secrets or handling them in an inappropriate manner, what security measures are mandated, and what options exist if you learn of a trade secret problem.

Controlling Future Technology Development by the Licensee—The "Grantback Paradox"

Before contemplating a license of your trade secrets and technology, a critical concept, particularly for high-tech companies, is the "Grantback Paradox." A grantback is a legal solution to the problem of what to do when new technologies are developed by a licensor or a licensee during the term of a license agreement. Assume that such developments were not foreseen by either licensor or licensee when the license was signed.

Two factual situations can arise. In one case, a licensee utilizes the technology obtained from a license. During the license term, the licensee independently develops a new application or a significant improvement on the licensed technology. Under the second scenario, a licensor, after transferring its technology to a licensee, develops an improved technology which the licensee would certainly have bargained for if it had existed. The reaction is identical in both cases— what rights does one party have in the other's new developments?

Guessing what new applications or technologies may develop in the future is akin to soothsaying. For purposes of illustration, imagine drawing a circle on a piece of paper and then licensing all the technology that is contained within the circle. A later-developed new technology might partially overlap the technology within the imaginary circle, while a second development, although in the same general field, may not touch on the licensed technology in the imaginary circle. Newly developed technologies may be true state-of-the-art advances or merely improvements on existing methods. One never knows until the development takes place.

Assume your company desires to license trade secret technology. Before initiating any inquiries seeking interested licensees, consider the following four factors:

Factor One: Have you clearly defined the technology to be licensed and its applications? This is always a more difficult job than it appears. Remember that you may license technology for all possible uses or for a limited purpose. For example, you may wish to license a trade secret chemical formulation only for use in the preparation of pharmaceutical products. If the license negotiations follow typical patterns, the "field of use" will be one of the last matters to be resolved. You will be under pressure to close the deal without going through the often tedious process of negotiating limitations on the use of the license. Generally, a broad application of licensed technology will lead to more difficulties in dealing with the grantback issue.

Factor Two: As the licensor of technology, do you expect to get the rights to any or all new developments the licensee may make on the technology during the term of the license agreement? You can forget a grantback analysis if receiving royalties is your sole goal. Most licensors, though, try to maintain at least some control over their technology even after it is licensed and undergoes further developments.

Factor Three: Assuming you have continuing interest in licensed technology, do you desire an option (exclusive or non-exclusive) or exclusive rights to after-developed improvements? Does it make a difference if the improvement is a mere modification, a state-of-the-art advance, or an innovation applicable to a new business sector? The key here is the degree of exclusivity and the scope of application of licensee's improvements and inventions.

Factor Four: As a condition of the original licensee, do you desire a grantback of the licensee's improvements at no cost or will you pay for them? If you pay for the rights (exclusive or non-exclusive), will this be negotiated at the time of disclosure or stipulated in the original contract? If you cannot agree on an appropriate royalty, what is done then?

The expressed concern about grantbacks should *not* be underestimated—particularly since where valuable trade secrets are part of the license, United States antitrust laws are involved. A grantback clause that is too broad can result in problems under those laws. Grantbacks viewed as "unreasonable" by courts are set aside and not enforced when challenged.

A scale of the varying degrees of antitrust exposure from badly written grantback clauses is illustrated in Figure One. On the other hand, grantbacks which are too narrowly drawn offer little protection. The trick is to find a proper balance. (See page 102.)

A grantback clause in a license agreement can be drafted in multiple ways—exclusive royalty-free grantback, exclusive grantback with negotiated royalty, non-exclusive royalty-free grantback, or non-exclusive option to negotiate—to name just a few options. The best advice to follow in working with your lawyer is to avoid overreaching in the grantback area. By licensing more narrowly, you are not as threatened by the grantback.

In conclusion, decide at an early point what is to be licensed, the scope of the license, the degree to which grantbacks of technology are desirable, and the type of grantback that will be legally enforceable. Do this analysis *before* approaching potential licensees and make it part of the initial licensing package. Evaluate the licensing benefits to see if they justify the overall risks of the loss of control over your trade secrets. The decision is rarely an easy one to make.

Figure One

TECHNOLOGY GRANTBACKS TO LICENSOR FROM LICENSEE— THE SCALE OF ANTITRUST RISKS

All Licensee improvements in all fields flow exclusively to licensor royalty-free*	All Licensee improvements in a narrow field of technology go exclusively to licensor royalty-free§	Licensor obtains a non-exclusive royalty free license for after-developed technologies§	Licensor has rights on a non-exclusive basis for a predetermined royalty of new technologies§	Licensor has first option to review and negotiate for rights to licensee's development+

*Exceptionally high antitrust risk

+No Antitrust risk

§Antitrust Exposure:
Must be evaluated based on:
1. Exclusivity as a factor
2. Amount to be paid for Technology
3. Reasonableness of restriction
4. Scope of the disclosure
5. Time period of disclosure
6. Value of Original License

102

The Five Stages of a Licensing Transaction

Like everything in life, a license transaction has a beginning, a middle, and an end. Trade secrets, if not handled properly, can be irrevocably lost at any stage.

Earlier chapters of this book presented methods of locating, valuing, and protecting trade secrets within the corporate structure. A licensing transaction is an entirely new type of situation. It demands very specific skills. Instead of tightly reigning in access to trade secrets by employees, agents, subcontractors, and other third parties, licensing requires a company to relinquish control over valuable trade secrets in exchange for royalties. Because of the nature of a license agreement, a licensor has less influence over the actions of the licensee and its employees, yet exactly the same dangers exist for trade secret disclosure in both circumstances.

To begin our analysis of the licensing process, we will make three basic assumptions. *First assumption*—your company desires to license valuable trade secrets, understands their true commercial value, and has genuine business reasons for seeking a licensing partner. *Second assumption*—you have undertaken a detailed evaluation of the risks of licensing to your company and reached a decision that the benefits of the right license outweigh both short- and long-term risks. *Third assumption*—you have carefully considered the grantback of after-developed technology and the methods for handling grantback questions have been resolved.

A licensing transaction can be broken into five stages. These are: locating potential licensees and evaluating their suitability, the prenegotiation secrecy agreement with a potential licensee, negotiating a trade secret licensing agreement, the key elements of the license agreement, and managing trade secrets during the license. The balance of this chapter will examine each step, concentrating on a single goal—protecting trade secrets from unauthorized use.

Stage One of the Licensing Transaction: Locating Potential Licensees and Evaluating Their Suitability

As incredible as it may seem, many companies conclude license agreements with the first licensee that knocks on their door. This is ironic since few companies would select an acquisition candidate in this way. A licensee is all too often a shot in the dark as opposed to a carefully planned decision. Why does a successful company with proven trade secret technology fail to license effectively? There is no one answer, but three techniques will contribute to increasing your chances for a successful search. Create a precise licensee profile, assign the job of locating and evaluating potential licensees to the right person, and establish a realistic time frame for the search process.

Creating the Licensee Profile

Your company must decide in advance exactly what qualities it desires in a licensee. Planning, not chance, should determine how the list of qualities is determined and what elimination procedures will be followed once candidates are found.

Start by preparing a licensee profile. Each licensee profile should consider at least the following five elements, defined and weighted according to their importance: financial strength, size of company and market position, geographic location, current level of technology, and suitability for continuing or cross-licensing opportunities. The use of the profile will permit a quantitative approach to reviewing potential licensees.

Financial Resources

The financial strength of a licensing partner is critical. Whether or not technology will be properly exploited depends to a great degree on capital availability of the licensee. Weakness in financial resources can undermine long-term goals and lead to serious problems, particularly in a multiyear license with royalties calculated on future sales.

Physical Size and Corporate Makeup

The physical size of a company and its market share in the relevant markets must be considered. A small company licensing its trade secrets should be quite careful before granting a license to a much larger company. The risk to the small business of creating a long-term competitor increases geometrically with the physical size and resources of the licensee. If your licensee is too big, your product may get lost in the shuffle, getting insufficient attention to succeed. On the other hand, a large company which is a market leader in its sector can usually offer a licensor greater long-term royalty revenue and a more lucrative upfront payment.

The difficulty in decision-making and ability to control trade secret dissemination throughout a corporation increases with the physical size of a company. A small licensor is often ill-equipped to force a large licensee to comply with secrecy requirements even if they are spelled out in a contract. Beyond that, if trade secrets have possible applications to a scope of activities broader than what was included in a license, a large licensee may attempt to use licensed trade secrets whether or not authorized. Consider a corporation with multiple divisions and groups. Licensing a large company normally compounds the risks of unintended trade secret exposure.

Geographic Location of Licensee

In creating a license profile, consider the geographic location of a target licensee. Often, entry into a new geographic area results in a search for a licensee. You should think about finding a company which in its current geographic location can produce the products and also effectively market them without the need for unusual efforts. Some important questions that must be answered are:

—Does the licensee offer sales coverage throughout the entire target geographic region?

—Is the production site placed advantageously relative to the key markets?

—Is the licensee active in other geographic areas outside the target territory?

—Is the licensee likely to become active in selling the licensed products in other markets before the licensor can become established?

—Can the licensee supply servicing and counseling after a sale where required?

Do not forget there are geographic areas of the United States which possess a higher overall degree of sensitivity to trade secrets and their realistic commercial value. This awareness can be a two-edged sword. For example, in Silicon Valley, California, without doubt, there exists a general appreciation of the value of trade secrets. This makes it conceptually easier to license trade secrets, but at the same time in this high-tech center there are greater risks of industrial espionage or unethical employees. As a result, all these geographic implications should be examined *before* a licensee is sought.

Technical Competence

It cannot be overemphasized that a licensor should decide in advance what level of technology it is willing to transfer to a licensee. The licensee must be equipped to apply the licensed technology. Some licensees do not have sufficient expertise to properly exploit licensed technology. Since most licensees insist on exclusive rights, the licensor may be prevented from seeking an alternative licensee if the initial licensee fails to properly apply the technology. Because royalties are most commonly calculated upon a per-unit-production basis, the long- and short-term return on the license may be adversely affected if the wrong type of licensee is chosen.

Ability to Cross-License

The last factor in creating a licensee profile is the decision whether a company is willing to license additional or new technology to the same licensee in the future. If the license is a one-shot deal, this factor is not relevant, but if a long-term relationship is anticipated by future additional licensing acquisitions, or joint venture, then careful attention is mandated. If a company with trade secrets is looking to bolster its own storehouse of technology in a particular area, approach possible licensees with the thought of locating potential partners who may be able to cross-license technology that a licensor needs.

How to Quantify Your License Profile for the Best Results

A rating system is helpful in evaluating potential licensees. The license profile should be quantified. One approach is to assign each of the five factors just discussed a ten-points maximum value. Rank the five factors according to their importance to your license proposal. Each potential license is rated on a maximum 50-points basis. With this quantitative approach, a licensee profile is created and can be objectively measured. After the raw data is calculated, then subjective criteria can be applied against potential licensees.

Who Is Most Qualified to Find Licensees?

Most companies look within their own ranks for the employee assigned to the job of locating licensees. Unfortunately, not all companies currently have an employee qualified to effectively conduct a detailed selection process. A search and evaluation of potential licensees conducted on a national or even international basis demands unique skills. Those skills are best developed in an experienced outside consultant. It is strongly recommended that the search process be handled by an outside consultant rather than one of your company's own employees.

An outside licensee consultant is preferable because a critical element in the selection process is objectivity. Since employees of companies are affected by the policies, personalities and politics within their own companies, their decisions are invariably influenced by a desire to benefit one part or division of a company over another. Employees will often seek a "safe" candidate as opposed to the right licensing partner who is harder to locate. The possibility of an employee's looking for the easy way out is a continuing risk. Equally important is the fact that in-house personnel normally are assigned to work on a number of projects. A licensee search is a project which will probably not receive the full and complete attention of an employee. Adequate financial or other motivations at the corporate level to insure personal attention to selecting licensees are almost invariably missing. The same rationale applies to companies which would attempt to use a foreign subsidiary of a related division to locate foreign licensing partners.

There is no easy method to track down potential licensees. Various companies in the United States and abroad offer for sale lists of electronic data banks of licensable technology. The difficulty with those lists is that only those potential licensees who are desperate for new products or diversification show up on them. The licensor, therefore, only comes into contact with firms that need inquiries and not necessarily with the most qualified potential licensees. The selection process is left to chance rather than a pragmatic licensee search.

There are at least three distinct advantages to employing a qualified licensing consultant. First, the consultant is able to make whatever level of time commitment is required to meet project goals. Second, the consultant can bring objectivity to the selection process. Third, the consultant can be forced to adhere to a strict time frame and to produce results within those requirements or be discharged.

Throughout the United States there are numerous "consultants" who bill themselves as "experts" in the licensing area. As a general rule, it is better to use consultants who charge an hourly, daily, or project rate than consultants who work on a percentage basis calculated on the value of the license if it is successfully concluded. Most consultants who work on a percentage basis will not conduct a search. They prefer, instead, to draw from licensing opportunities already known and available to them. Only the easy assignments are fulfilled and only the easy-to-find licensee candidates are considered. Some United States manufacturing companies have been burned so often by commission consultants and brokers that they automatically refuse any contact with a commissioned consultant or broker.

It is far preferable to pay a consultant on an hourly or project basis and then to break the project into various elements and pay only upon successful completion of each section. If one section is not handled well, a new consultant is retained for the balance of the work.

Five-Step Procedure to Locate a Licensee

Although there is no single method guaranteed to locate the proper licensee, there are a number of approaches that have proved highly effective. One successful method is the product of Suter Associates, Inc., a Management Consultant for Technology Transfer and Market Entry which is located in Pittsburgh, Pennsylvania. This method consists of a five-step procedure leading to the commencement of negotiations with a single potential licensing partner. It is recommended that a licensing consultant be given a maximum six-month period to accomplish all five steps. The length of time required for each individual step depends on the particular trade secrets involved. While this technique has been developed by the outside consultant, it can be adapted for implementation by in-house personnel.

Step One—Collecting Background Information on the Licensor

The first step is to collect complete background information on your company and its activities as the proposed licensor. This includes an evaluation of existing technology to be transferred and a complete evaluation of your company's capabilities. The purpose is to ensure that the licensing consultant is totally informed on all aspects of your company. Remember, the consultant will be acting as your salesman.

He needs all the sales tools and ammunition a salesman requires before attacking a new territory. You should initially assign one or more of your employees to deal with the licensing consultant so that questions and information requests can be quickly resolved.

It is strongly recommended that before you supply even general background information to the licensing consultant, the licensing consultant be required to execute a secrecy agreement binding it to your company. If your licensing consultant is a corporation, all key employees who will have access to your trade secret information should be made to sign individual secrecy agreements.

All documentary information made available from the licensor to your licensing consultant should be prominently marked on each page. An example of a trade secret notice is:

<u>TRADE SECRET</u>

THIS DOCUMENT CONTAINS TRADE SECRET INFORMA- TION OF _____ COMPANY. THIS DOCUMENT IS DIS- CLOSED TO _____ IN ITS CAPACITY AS A LICENSING CONSULTANT WHO IS BOUND BY A SECRECY AGREEMENT. _____ IS NOT AUTHORIZED WITHOUT SPECIFIC WRIT- TEN CONSENT TO DISCLOSE THIS DOCUMENT OR ITS CON- TENTS TO ANY OTHER PERSON. CIVIL AND/OR CRIMINAL PROSECUTIONS WILL BE INITIATED AGAINST VIOLATORS.

Step Two—Preparation of the License Prospectus

The consultant will prepare the License Prospectus based on the background information for presentation to prospective licensee candidates. The license prospectus is a selective marketing approach designed to make all relevant information available to possible licens- ees. It will enable companies to make an initial evaluation on whether they wish to enter into licensing negotiations. Be sure the licensing prospectus is professionally produced and contains a detailed table of contents, an introduction expressing the intentions of the licensor, and the points described in the preceding paragraphs. This is a very serious document that does not require the gloss of sales literature. It is recommended that each licensing brochure be individually numbered or coded in such a way so that its distribution is limited. This way, specific copies may be tracked down at any point. Indiscriminate distribution of brochures will only lead to problems. Although each licensing prospectus will be drafted to meet the requirements of the particular client, there are a number of common elements.

The license prospectus—background on licensor

A licensing prospectus must present an overview of the history of the proposed licensor. This would include a detailed discussion of company structure and operations. Beyond that, a license prospectus should describe the current management lineup of the licensor and its line of products or activities. It is recommended that the prospectus clearly state early in the document that the licensing consultant representing the licensor is being paid entirely by the licensor, and no fee will be due to the licensing consultant from the licensee if the transaction is successfully concluded.

The license prospectus—detailed description of licensed products or technology

The licensing prospectus should describe in detail the products or processes of the licensor employing the trade secrets to be licensed. Where a line of products is produced by the trade secrets, the present uses of those products and their geographic distribution may be relevant. Other information such as current market share of licensor and prospects of future growth should be made available.

The license prospectus—the trade secrets to be disclosed

Finally, the licensing prospectus must give a generalized description of the trade secret information available for license. It should also state if additional technology will be available from the licensor if a license is successfully concluded. Under no circumstances should any trade secret information be included with the prospectus. Trade secrets can only be transferred if additional requirements are met. The point of the prospectus is merely to locate interested potential partners.

Step Three—How to Locate the Broadest Range of Potential Licensees

The greatest single value of a licensing consultant lies in the ability to locate all potential licensees for particular trade secrets. The licensing consultant will review the factors of financial strength, geographic location, size and market position of the potential licensee, current level of technology, and desire for continuing or cross-license opportunities, and then seek out the broadest range of potential licensees with the license prospectus.

Each consultant has its own methods of developing comprehensive lists of potential licensees. Initially, you should direct the consultant to define the total universe of candidates. This process can take from one to three months depending on what is being licensed. Once the largest possible list has been obtained, the Licensee Profile is set off against the list of potential licensees and the elimination procedure begins.

An actual example may help illustrate how Steps 1, 2 and 3 work. A European company with technology, with possible applications in the United States automobile industry, available for license for sale to original equipment manufacturers (OEM) was reviewing its options. Although this company was actively engaged in selling its products through original equipment manufacturers in the European market, it had not yet penetrated the United States market. A United States license consultant was hired on an hourly basis to locate potential licensees. The consultant first spent one month learning everything about the licensor and then prepared a License Prospectus. After the Prospectus was approved by the European company, the licensing consultant defined the criteria and then was able to locate across the United States more than seven hundred potential licensees by researching various sources. Note that no direct contacts were yet initiated. Once the comprehensive list of potential licensees was compiled, the elements contained in the Licensee Profile were applied against all companies on the list. In this case, the licensor wanted a licensee of between twenty-five and one hundred million dollars in sales, manufacturing capabilities for both precision ferrous metalworking and plastic forming, a strong capital base, and a geographic location in the mid-Atlantic or central United States region. A potential licensee also needed existing contacts with the major United States automobile manufacturers. When those elements were applied to the seven hundred potential licensees, the list was reduced to approximately one hundred possible licensees.

In the actual example just described, the licensing consultant took a total of three weeks work over three months to do the following: month #1—do background study of the licensor and write a profile; month #2—assemble the master list, and month #3—refine the list by applying the criteria provided by the European company. Therefore, in just three months, a manageable list was obtained at reasonable cost, and Step 4 was ready to be implemented.

Step Four—The First Contact with Licensee Candidates

After completing Steps 1, 2 and 3, your company should possess a manageable list of real prospects. At this point a carefully designed personalized letter should be sent out to all potential licensees on the refined list. The letter should be directed to the specific individual who is most responsible in his company for acquiring new technology. Targeting the decision-maker is essential.

Ten days after the initial letters go out, the consultant will follow up with a telephone call to the recipients of the letters. The Licensing Prospectus will be forwarded only to those companies which express interest in the proffered licensee oportunity at the time of the telephone call. Within three weeks thereafter, those potential licensees who are sent the Prospectus are contacted once again. After studying the Prospectus, some candidates will decline the offer. The list again narrows.

Step Five—The Elimination Process—Winnowing the Potential Licensees

When a limited list of licensees is identified, the consultant should carefully check out the best prospects without directly requesting information from them. Now the Licensee Profile originally developed should again be matched against the potential candidates. If possible, develop a quantitative approach. Although it is possible to carry on negotiations with a number of companies simultaneously, it is not advisable. This is particularly true when your company will reveal trade secret information in the course of license negotiations. Pick out the two or three most likely prospects. Initiate a face-to-face meeting with each. Based upon the results of those meetings select a single licensee candidate to initiate negotiations with. Under no circumstances should any trade secrets be revealed at this point. It is here you face the first of many risks to your trade secrets as the negotiations are set to proceed.

Stage Two of the Licensing Transaction: The Secrecy Agreement—Pre-negotiation Requirement

The single most critical stage of licensing trade secrets occurs on the initial contact with the potential licensee with whom negotiations are to commence. By this point a detailed check should have been made of the target company's reputation, financial strength, market share, and potential competitiveness and a decision reached that negotiations will begin.

It is absolutely essential that each potential licensee sign a pre-negotiation secrecy agreement *before* any trade secret information is revealed. Remember, your potential licensee has already had the opportunity to review the Licensing Prospectus and decided on at least general terms it is interested in your technology which is available for license. Again, the theme of this book is that trade secrets, to maintain their proprietary and secret character, can not be revealed except under the most carefully controlled conditions. Although an oral promise from a potential licensee not to reveal trade secrets is technically an enforceable legal obligation, the preferable method under all circumstances is a written secrecy agreement signed *before* disclosure.

At this stage as licensor you are saying to your potential licensee "I have valuable industrial trade secrets and I am willing to license them to you for a price that is quite reasonable." Your licensee's reaction is, "I will be glad to take a look at the trade secrets and if I like them, I will be glad to pay a reasonable price." The universal problem facing licensors is to reveal the secrets and yet control them in the event that a license agreement is not ultimately executed.

In almost every case, the potential licensee's technical personnel must evaluate the trade secrets before rendering an opinion that the licensing of the trade secrets is desirable and that the licensing price is reasonable. The pre-negotiation secrecy agreement allows the trade secrets to be examined by the potential licensee only for the purpose of studying their value. Timing is a critical factor in a pre-disclosure secrecy agreement and the disclosure must be strictly tied to a limited time period. A number of key elements and considerations for a pre-disclosure secrecy agreement are discussed in the following paragraphs.

Defining Proprietary and Trade Secrecy Information

Although the Licensing Prospectus will contain general references to the trade secret information to be conveyed, the pre-disclosure secrecy agreement must define the exact information to be discussed during negotiations. Trade secret information should be physically segregated from other general types of information to be disclosed. This initial segregation will simplify the procedure for marking documents and providing for their handling.

Who Is to Sign the Secrecy Agreement?

Not all people who work for a corporation are empowered to bind the corporation to a contract. Be sure that the proper officer or manager within a corporation signs the pre-disclosure agreement. This will help to avoid legal challenges later and will draw attention at the executive level of a potential licensee to the importance of the license negotiations. The secrecy agreement is an integral part. For the American company dealing outside the United States, it may not be immediately obvious who can and cannot bind a company. Likewise, the non-United States company seeking licensees is often mystified by titles such as General Manager, Operations Director, Vice President, Director for the Division, Executive Vice President, Chief Executive Officer, or Chief Operating Officer.

The Risks of the Large Corporation Licensee

The conglomerate or large corporation licensee presents special problems. The multiple divisions of such a licensee may desire to apply your trade secrets or technology to a variety of different and distinct uses, only some of which you may intend to benefit. The key is to avoid the indiscriminate disclosure of your trade secrets beyond a defined circle of need. It is critical in your initial pre-negotiation secrecy agreement to state that the "scope" of the license is limited to a specific use by a particular division or subsidiary of the licensee. Where a licensee has other divisions or subsidiaries seeking your trade secrets for application to additional uses, require a second disclosure agreement to be signed by the other divisions or subsidiaries, providing an independent basis for royalties earned.

In the example just given, it is best to have the division president or appropriate top officer of a subsidiary personally execute the secrecy agreement. While this won't create personal liability, it will establish an awareness of the importance of the disclosure. The legal department of the parent corporation should be independently notified that the disclosure is limited both in scope and to a particular corporate entity and may not be further disclosed.

In addition, clearly state in the pre-disclosure secrecy agreement that your potential licensee will not make your trade secrets available to the general public or third parties under *any* circumstances without your written permission. Obviously, there will be no problem if a license agreement is later executed. But in the event negotiations fail, this obligation must be completely clear and unambiguous in the initial secrecy agreement.

Controlling the Conduct of Potential Licensees and Their Employees

Regardless of who the potential licensee is, the secrecy agreement should designate those specific employees who are authorized to examine your trade secrets for evaluation purposes. Specifically, the secrecy agreement must provide that no non-employee of the potential licensee will have access to trade secrets without your prior written consent. If bankers and non-company advisors such as accountants and lawyers are needed in the evaluation process, demand that they be identified and, where possible, required to sign individual non-disclosure agreements. Try to create a paper trail of non-disclosure or secrecy agreements which exist wherever your trade secrets go. In the event of a subsequent unauthorized use of your trade secrets or if they somehow become available to the public, the ability to show that all reasonable efforts were taken at each stage is critical if a court's help is expected.

Asking for Individual Employee Secrecy Agreements

Where reasonable, require each employee who reviews trade secret information to sign a brief one- or two-page "Employees Secrecy Agreement." This agreement will provide a basis for legal action in the event of disclosure. In addition, having the employee sign a specific secrecy agreement underscores the critical nature of the trade secrets he is reviewing. It is a reminder of the personal liability he can incur if he discloses the trade secrets. A one-page secrecy agreement can go a long way in educating employees about the dangers of careless handling or intentional disclosure of trade secrets.

The Time Period the Secrecy Agreement Is Valid

The pre-disclosure secrecy agreement should allow a potential licensee a limited period of time in which to review and evaluate the proffered trade secrets. The disclosure should not exceed 60 to 90 days. Longer review periods make it more difficult to isolate the trade secrets from the everyday workings and knowledge pool of potential licensees and their employees. Initial secrecy agreements signed by individual employees will lose their psychological impact over time. The likelihood that non-authorized people will either gain or be given access to the trade secrets also increases with time.

One approach is to tie the disclosure to an option. The license option is purchased from a licensor by a potential licensee. During the option period, the licensee candidate blocks a licensor from offering a license to any other candidate within the territory.

The Licensor's Right to Injunctive Relief Against Violators

In many cases, the licensor is far more concerned, at least in the short-term, with stopping any further unauthorized disclosure than in seeking money damages. An injunction issued by a court is a specific order directing someone to do something or to stop doing something. A pre-disclosure secrecy agreement should grant your company the right to seek immediate injunctive relief and to obtain that relief in the court most accessible to your company.

The Liquidated Damages Approach to Damages

Proof of actual damages suffered as a result of contract breach is time-consuming, costly and difficult. The purpose of the pre-disclosure secrecy agreement is to avoid litigation by making the parties reach a common understanding of the needs and requirements of non-disclosure. Nevertheless, the agreement can be breached, and if breached, litigation will result. It is particularly difficult to prove what type and the extent of damages (in monetary terms) that occurred as a result of wrongful disclosure of your trade secrets.

One solution to this problem is to include a "liquidated damages provision" in the secrecy agreement. This establishes in advance the specific dollar figure that must be paid if there is a violation of the contract. The legal enforceability of such a provision varies from state to state. Even if not enforceable, in whole or in part, such a provision is a powerful psychological tool to impress upon potential licensees the seriousness with which you will treat any violation of secrecy obligations.

The Procedures for Marking of Trade Secret Documents

Once a pre-disclosure secrecy agreement is signed and before trade secret information is transmitted, mark all documents clearly as trade secret information which is covered by a secrecy agreement. Earlier in this chapter, specific language was proposed. When a large volume of documents is delivered, each page of all the documents should be consecutively numbered. Keep an index of all documents transmitted that contain trade secret information. It is advisable to request a receipt signed by the potential licensee acknowledging that information was received. Be sure receipts are specific as to the documents released. Where possible, maintain records of when and to whom oral trade secret information was transmitted. If a dispute arises later, following these procedures assures that there will be no question which documents were disclosed.

Stage Three of the Licensing Transaction: Trade Secrets and the Negotiation Process

Sixty to ninety days after the pre-disclosure secrecy agreement is signed and trade secrets transferred, it should be clear whether substantive negotiations will occur. The licensing negotiation process should have a defined beginning and end. When possible, stipulate strict time limits for the total negotiation before negotiations start. Extensions of the negotiating time frame are granted later only for good reason and confirmed in writing. Normally, it is to the licensee's advantage to delay consummating negotiations until *all* possible questions have been answered, and the licensee has fully evaluated the trade secrets of the licensor. Where trade secrets are involved in a process or product with a limited commercial life, time is even more critical for the licensor. Therefore, strict adherence to scheduling is a prerequisite.

In license transactions of trade secrets there are two basic matters to be negotiated. First, key policy matters such as royalties, grantbacks, and the term of the license which a top-level corporate person has to make a decision on. The second half of the negotiation occurs at the technical level where engineering and technical staff of the potential licensee must be convinced the trade secrets are of genuine value. At an early negotiation stage, key technical people of the potential licensor should be matched with their counterparts. A line of communication should be opened immediately so that technical questions are answered on a continuing basis. This avoids technical glitches after major policy points have been resolved.

A valuable technique to move negotiations along as quickly as possible is to arrange for top-level representatives for each side to meet at the beginning of the negotiation process. Since there are key policy decisions that must be overcome before a license agreement can be reduced to writing, these decisions require initial involvement of top-level corporate decision makers. Leaving major policy issues to the end, such as royalties or grantbacks of technology, is almost always a mistake.

Major Non-Technical Points to Be Resolved by Negotiation

Exclusive or Non-Exclusive License to Trade Secrets

The scope of rights to trade secrets is a key conceptual problem. Although the license prospectus already shown to potential licensees should state whether exclusive or non-exclusive rights to the trade secrets are offered, negotiations often produce differences between the parties. Invariably, a licensor attempts to maintain some control over trade secrets even though the secrets are ostensibly being offered for an exclusive license to the other party. In negotiating with a potential licensee, carefully explain the breadth of the proposed license. Where possible, avoid the use of the terms "exclusive" or "non-exclusive" in the license. Unless very clear definitions are offered, ambiguities or uncertainties are normally construed against the licensor by courts.

A better approach is to enumerate during negotiations and in documents the applications for the trade secrets. If reasonable, give examples of the applications. For instance, if a particular chemical formulation for use in a pesticide is available for license, the license should define the specific rights granted to the chemical formulation. If the chemical formulation also has applications to non-pesticide industries, defining the uses for which it is offered can avoid later disputes between licensor and licensee.

Do not ignore the varying tax consequences resulting from the licensing of trade secrets. Have the application of United States tax laws to trade secret transfers evaluated by a tax lawyer or tax accountant *before* entering into negotiations. Depending on the type of rights transferred and whether they are exclusive or non-exclusive, the tax treatment of the royalty payments can be viewed as ordinary income or, in some cases, capital gains. By deciding ahead of time what the ultimate objective is, structuring the license is easier and tax problems minimized. When licensing overseas, remember you will confront both United States and foreign tax implications. Many countries have bilateral tax treaties with the United States which limit the tax bite that can be levied on royalties by tax authorities.

The Maintenance of Trade Secrets

After a potential licensing partner completes an initial evaluation of your trade secrets, it is common to receive additional requests during negotiations for more information. Since the potential licensee is trying to evaluate the uniqueness of your trade secrets, particularly if a long-term licensing agreement is contemplated, the potential licensee may seek the opinion of outside experts.

Be cautious about disclosures of your trade secrets to parties who are not employees of the company with which you are negotiating. Every time your trade secrets leave your immediate circle of control, the risk of their disclosure to other third parties increases geometrically. You must insist upon individual secrecy agreements binding any outside parties who evaluate your trade secrets. This applies to outside consultants, bankers, accountants, lawyers, consultants, or subcontractors. Insist upon prior written notice from a potential licensee *before* the trade secrets are revealed to any outside parties. Such notice will provide you with adequate opportunity to request secrecy agreements to be signed or to veto the request if necessary. As a condition of permission to disclose, ask for the reasons behind the disclosure and the scope of the disclosure. Evaluate the reasons before deciding to grant permission.

Be aware of the possibilities of conflicts of interest in third parties. By the time you have entered into negotiations with a potential licensee, risks of conflicts of interest from that quarter are small. However, outside lawyers, accountants, consultants, and subcontractors may deal with potential competitors of your company and are a conflict danger. The purpose of a secrecy agreement binding the outside parties is as much educational as it is legal. When lawyers talk, they often refer to a concept known as the "Chinese Wall." This is a situation where a law firm possesses secret information from one client which if known would put it in conflict with another existing client of the law firm. The procedure within the law firm directs one lawyer not to mention what he knows to other lawyers in the firm about a sensitive issue. This is known as building a "Chinese Wall." Chinese wall mentality is dangerous and is to be avoided. Forcing secrecy agreements on outside third parties with access to your trade secrets is a good method for flushing out potential conflict problems that lead to unauthorized disclosure of your trade secrets.

When documents containing your trade secrets are transmitted to a potential licensee, each document should carry a clear warning on its face that the document is trade secret information and violators are subject to serious penalties. It is critical that warnings and notices appear on every piece of related policy and technical information including raw data, specifications, blueprints, test data, correspondence, or any other unpatented information that you consider trade secrets. Failure to mark your documents consistently creates an impression that information *not* marked is not to be viewed as trade secret information.

During negotiations, maintain a list of the trade secret documents produced and advise your potential licensor whether copies are permitted and where original documents and copies are to be physically retained. In the event the negotiations fall through unexpectedly, you need the ability to locate all trade secret documents and copies quickly. When litigation is required, any court is more amenable to forcing return of documents if their location can be reasonably ascertained. In the case of court-ordered seizure, knowing exactly where the documents are located is critical.

The Grantback of Technology

Initial decisions on grantback philosophy for new technology applications or after discovered technologies by the licensor or licensee are an important part of negotiations. Since the United States antitrust laws prohibit overly severe restrictions on grantbacks, analyze whether a conceptual agreement between both parties raises the unwanted specter of antitrust. To repeat, the general rule is that it is better to license more narrowly and by a defined field of use than it is to offer a totally broad and exclusive royalty-free grantback to the licensor for antitrust reasons.

Negotiations and the Technical Phase Problems

A technical phase negotiation is carried out simultaneously while non-technical conceptual points are resolved. The technical aspects of a license are a potential mine field unless special care is taken. Often, trade secret licenses fail, not because the legal contract is inadequate, but because there are misconceptions at the technical level of what specific trade secrets are actually being transmitted. It is advisable for non-technical negotiators to consult on a continuing basis with the technical staff to assure that what is being bargained for will actually be delivered. Appendices to trade secret license agreements contain technical points and standards. The standards should be prepared with care and understood by both sides before an agreement is finalized.

It is not unusual for a license to provide for continuing technical advice and consultation through the life of the license. The licensor has to be cautious not to commit itself through the negotiation process to expand the scope of what was originally anticipated. The broader the continuing disclosure, the greater the risk to trade secrets.

Make specific stipulations in your agreement that no oral transfers of trade secret information occur between the technical personnel and any outsiders without permission. Technical people are particularly susceptible to revealing information without directly understanding the threat that it poses to trade secrets.

A helpful technique is for the licensor to prepare a checklist of "do's and don't's"approved by both parties at the beginning of the negotiating process. This document is then given to all employees of a potential licensee including technical personnel with access to the licensor's trade secret information. This procedure should help to reinforce the importance of controlling trade secrets among those with access at the early stage.

What to Do If the License Negotiations Collapse

To prevent negotiations from dragging on, set rigid time limits in advance for the completion of certain activities such as licensee evaluation of disclosed trade secrets. At some point it may become clear that the negotiations will not be successful. If an agreement is not possible, terminate negotiations cleanly. The first step is to send formal written notification to your negotiating partner that negotiations are at an end. This will act as a benchmark for future relationships between the parties. The important thing is to create a clear date from which negotiations are viewed as terminated.

Simultaneously with written notification that negotiations are over, demand in writing the return of all trade secret documents and information transferred up to that point. It is best that top officials of the potential licensee are notified personally by letter. This demand must ask for any and all copies of every document and item, trade secret or not, that was shown to the potential partner. If, as recommended, all documents were consecutively numerically marked, it will be a simple matter to check if at least one complete set is returned. Beyond that, as part of the predisclosure secrecy agreement, all copies go to the licensor upon demand. Continually impress on your former negotiating partner that it has no right to retain any copies, regardless of the reason. If there are several possible depositories for trade secrets at the potential licensee's places of business, send an appropriate notification and warning letter to each of those locations with a demand for return of original documents and copies. The need to reclaim information is the reason why it was suggested earlier that the licensor at all times should keep track of what information is conveyed and where it is sent during negotiations. With the rise of information being placed in electronic storage mechanisms and with easy transmission, the problem becomes more serious and difficult to contend with.

Direct formal written notices should be sent to all those individuals who have signed individual secrecy agreements during the course of negotiations advising them of the end of negotiations. These notices should warn each individual he is *personally* bound to maintain the secrecy of those trade secret documents even though negotiations terminated. Include in the notice a request to the employee that any original documents or copies in his possession be returned. Consider asking if any of the information has been placed in an electronic storage mechanism and where the storage bank is physically located. Such a notice places an affirmative legal duty on the employee to take action if he has reason to believe his employer has not complied with the request to return all documents. In the event trade secrets leak after cessation of negotiations, this legal notice to employees will provide a proper excuse to join employees individually as parties to a lawsuit on trade secret disclosure if you have reason to believe they have mishandled trade secrets.

Send written notice of negotiation termination to all third parties who had access to your trade secret information during the course of negotiations. For this purpose, knowledge of the existence of all third parties is essential during the course of negotiations. Otherwise, effective notice at this point is impossible. The legal notice to outsiders of their potential personal liability will act as an additional pressure on your former negotiating partner to comply with the requirements of the secrecy agreement.

After the dust settles and all documents are returned, you are not finished. Since your potential partner had access to your important trade secrets, it is recommended you observe its activities for some period of time. Naturally, the amount of effort will depend upon the value and nature of the trade secrets which had been revealed. First, look for new product introduction by the potential licensee which might in some way be related to your trade secret information revealed during the course of the negotiations. By a process of reverse engineering or careful inspection, it should become clear if your trade secrets have been wrongfully appropriated. Second, try to find out if your former potential licensing partner subsequently entered into any licensing agreements or joint ventures with your potential competitors or companies who possess trade secret information similar to yours. The fear is that insights gained from access to your information may be used against you in future licensing activities by others. Even from a non-confidential standpoint, examinations of your operations, activities and planning revealed during the negotiation process can be damaging. And third, check where possible whether key top employees of your former licensing negotiation partner have left their employer and started their own companies. This source of trouble, even though it isn't from your former potential licensing partner, can be devastating. After two years if nothing has shown up, you are probably in the clear.

Stage Four of the Licensing Transaction: Important Concepts in the License Agreement

Too often, negotiations become snarled on just a few points that appear to be critical at a particular time. As a result, major points are ignored. Numerous factors are important in drafting a comprehensive license agreement. To be sure all important items are covered, including tax and antitrust aspects, a knowledgeable licensing lawyer should be consulted throughout the course of the negotiation stage of a license agreement. This section will highlight twelve concepts which the non-lawyer negotiator involved in the licensing of trade secrets should keep in mind. Before negotiations are concluded, review to see that the twelve areas are covered in the licensing agreement or understand the reasons why one or more of the points are not included.

Concept One—The Whereas Clauses

Licensing agreements frequently contain "Whereas" clauses. The Whereas Clause establishes the general understandings and contemplation of the parties at the moment the license agreement is signed. While some lawyers advise their clients "Whereas Clauses" in licensing agreements serve no purpose, the better view is that a licensor wants to frame in the clearest possible fashion the attitude of both parties at the time a licensing agreement is executed.

For example, a whereas clause referring to "valuable trade secret information" of the "licensor" which "will enable the licensee to enter into a new field of business" is an acknowledgement by the licensee of the true value and unique nature of the information received. This clause could be helpful at a later point if litigation arises. It would be difficult for the licensee to contend in court that the information of the licensor was not a trade secret or not of important commercial value as a defense to non-payment. Carefully drafted whereas clauses can be evidence of intent in court where the substantive contract is in dispute and not clear.

Concept Two—The Parties to the Agreement

The license contract must define and bind all parties to the license agreement. Although it appears obvious, mistakes have been made by executing a licensing agreement with a wholly owned subsidiary or division of another company without thought being given to the consequences.

If a division of a larger company is licensed and the other divisions want the licensed trade secrets or if a parent or related corporation of a subsidiary desires access to the licensed trade secrets, there is a genuine threat to the integrity of the trade secrets. Unless the license agreement specifically limits trade secret dissemination to the company or entity signing the license, there may well be problems. Specifically, if trade secrets licensed to one division of a company are transferred to another division, the license agreement should clearly authorize such transfers. When an intra-company transfer is authorized, it must be clear that the restrictions in the license contract are such that the same restraints apply to other divisions of the same company as in the original license. When you can anticipate that a related or parent company desires the information from the trade secret license agreement, it is strongly recommended you make the related or parent company become signators to the license contract. In the event trade secrets are disclosed to the parent later, this will preclude any legal arguments that a court has no jurisdiction over the conduct of the parent or related company.

Concept Three—Exclusivity and the Assignment of Rights

Clarity in the license is essential in defining whether or not rights to trade secrets are to be "exclusive" or "non-exclusive" and what that means. Exclusivity can have many meanings such as the use of trade secrets by geographic areas or referring to the particular applications which the licensed trade secrets may be put to in the production process. The earlier example of licensing of trade secrets for a chemical manufacturing process for sale in pesticides is applicable here. The power to assign rights under a license is equally important. The best approach is that trade secrets are not assignable to any other party unless specifically authorized in writing by the licensor. Freedom to assign can be a real problem where a licensee company desires to use a subcontractor to manufacture a specific item and trade secrets are disclosed. There, the trade secrets will be in the hands of a third party with all of the possible risks of authorized disclosure. Therefore, avoid all chance of assignment by a definitive licensing contract.

Concept Four—The Licensor as Consultant

When trade secrets are transferred by a license, the agreement may contain provisions for training and ongoing consultation services from licensor to licensee. If, as part of the deal, services and consultation are provided by licensor to licensee, limit the period of time and quantity of services the licensor is obligated to give. Assume a company agrees to license a turnkey lock-manufacturing facility. In the license, you would state that after the plant began commercial production, technical consulting from licensor to licensee would be provided at no cost for the first six months of the license. However, there is a maximum consultation in six months by two of the licensor's employees of ten working days. For anything beyond the initial free consultation, the license should state that the licensor is only to perform upon payment at a daily or hourly rate. Factor in daily or hourly charges, the amounts needed to cover in-house clerical functions and other indirect costs. Lawyers, doctors, and consultants are usually better at valuing their time on an incremental time basis than are businessmen in non-service industries who are conditioned to selling products or handling transactional business matters. Do not overlook consultant services as a profit center opportunity under the license.

Concept Five—The Individual Secrecy Agreement

Negotiate for the right to demand at your sole option that all employees of the licensee with access to your confidential information be required to sign individual secrecy agreements. Under the license agreement, the licensor should automatically be entitled to receive the names of all the licensee's employees who will work with your trade secret information as well as the names of any outside third parties. The license agreement should specifically prohibit any outside third party from examining any licensed trade secret information prior to notice to your company and, where desirable, the execution of an individual secrecy agreement. The right of the licensor to insist upon these conditions is very important and cannot be overemphasized.

Concept Six—Identification of Trade Secrets

All trade secret information which is transferred to a licensee should contain an appropriate marking. Consider inserting in the license agreement the exact language (warning) that will appear on all trade secret documents. For the information contained in documents which will later be rewritten or incorporated in the information banks of the licensee, proscribe if and how this is to be permitted. Even when the information is inputted into the licensee's computerized data bank, a warning "Trade Secret Information—Not to Be Disclosed" should be in the computer software so that the warning will appear every time the information is accessed. In some cases you may want to require your licensee to limit by computer entry code those individuals who will have access to your trade secret information. The level of safety precautions will certainly depend upon the value of your trade secrets—for valuable trade secrets such a step should not be viewed as burdensome by either the licensee or the licensor.

Concept Seven—Dealing with Grantbacks of Technology

The grantback clause is an essential element of any license. The grantback defines what new inventions, improvements, or ideas developed by the licensee during the term of the license the licensor is entitled to. It can also apply to future activities of the licensor. The grantback clause must state whether or not a licensor has an "exclusive" right to the improvements of the licensee and whether or not a royalty or compensation is due the licensee for new technological developments. Remember, United States antitrust laws can create problems in this area if the grantback is overly restrictive on the licensee.

Concept Eight—The Access to Licensee's Books and Records

A licensor of trade secret information needs the legal right of access to the business records of the licensee and ought to request it in the agreement. Quality and quantity control of products or processes produced from trade secrets are key factors in determining what royalties are owed the licensor. Beyond calculation of royalties, some licenses restrict the scope of use for trade secrets. A license agreement guaranteeing access to a licensee's records is a mechanism for the licensor. Without litigation, the licensor can evaluate whether or not the trade secrets are being used improperly in a manner broader than the underlying license permits. Inclusion of this provision permits a licensor to examine a licensee's operation periodically without initially raising suspicions about the true nature of the investigation. Contract provisions authorizing periodic physical visits by the licensor to the licensee's plant are also helpful.

Concept Nine—Cooperative Activities of Licensor and Licensee

Every license agreement must contain an affirmative covenant for licensor-licensee cooperation to halt patent, trademark, or trade secret infringement by any outsider who is not a party to the license agreement. Regardless of the reasons why trade secrets were wrongfully disclosed and who is at fault, a licensor has to be able to act immediately in a direct manner when threats to trade secrets exist. The ability to point to a particular provision in a license agreement forcing an instantaneous response and cooperation from a licensee is invaluable. As a side benefit, such a contract provision will reinforce in the licensee's mind the commercial value of trade secrets and create the possibility for a genuinely cooperative relationship.

Concept Ten—Force Majeure and Licensing

Contracts contain a "force majeure clause," otherwise known as an "Act of God Provision." Be quite careful in the wording of a force majeure clause where you are the licensor of trade secrets. Do not allow your lawyer to insert a standard force majeure clause that comes straight from a legal form book. Because of the critical nature of the continuing obligation by the licensee to protect the confidentiality of trade secrets, the force majeure clause must avoid any loopholes permitting a wayward licensee to escape liability claiming that an unforeseen "Act of God" caused a disclosure of trade secrets.

Concept Eleven—Termination of the License Agreement

One of the most critical provisions of a licensing contract deals with termination of the agreement. Every contract should state that the bankruptcy, insolvency, or other financial difficulty experienced by a licensee is without question an adequate basis for the licensor to declare the license terminated and to demand return of all trade secrets. The problem is more complicated when it is the licensor who is having financial problems. Consider including contract language permitting termination of a license and the mandatory return of trade secrets if the quality of the goods produced is not up to an identifiable standard. If this provision is included in the contract, it must be quantifiable by a formula or other objective means, the formula or mechanism part of the agreement. Stipulating the products produced by a licensee must meet the "approval" of the licensor, without something more definitive, will create more legal problems than it solves.

Concept Twelve—The Life of Secrecy Agreements

The license agreement should acknowledge and reaffirm all pre-existing secrecy obligations of the licensee. Assume for a moment the licensee signed a secrecy agreement at the beginning of negotiations. Is that agreement still valid and enforceable after the license agreement is signed? The danger is that an imprecisely written license contract can void the prior secrecy obligations of parties. Clear contract language is crucial. Also, in the event there is a premature termination of the license agreement at some future point, the license agreement must provide that secrecy provisions contained in the license agreement survive the termination of the agreement and continue to be enforceable against the licensee and all others. Otherwise, the termination of the licensing agreement might terminate the obligations of the licensee to hold trade secrets in confidence. That could be catastrophic.

Stage Five of the Licensing Transaction: Trade Secrets During the License Term

Traditionally, once a license agreement is signed there is little need for contact between licensor and licensee as long as royalties are paid in a timely fashion. The licensing relationship is not one of close contact like a joint venture. However, your company should view the licensing relation differently when valuable trade secrets are the core of the license. Unless trade secrets have a very brief prospective commercial life, you need a continuing interest in maintaining the confidential nature of trade secrets. An unfortunate aspect of many licensing transactions is that regardless of the contractual language, the licensee believes it has "bought" the trade secrets and so doesn't consider it owes any further responsibilities to a licensor as long as royalties are paid.

Sophisticated licensors develop and use internal corporate procedures to identify, control, implement, and store trade secrets. You should require that by specific license provision during the term of the agreement the licensee will follow similar procedures while handling the licensor's trade secrets. You should also insist the procedures to be followed in the licensee's dealings with subcontractors, suppliers, consultants, and agents are similar to yours. Establishing regular meetings with the licensee are a method by which informal checks are possible on the licensee's conduct. For example, if the license agreement sets up semiannual meetings between the licensor and licensee, the licensee will learn to expect and accept continuing inquiries by the licensor on secrecy agreements compliance. Developing a close, personal relationship between the licensor and licensee helps to foster this attitude.

Keeping track of a licensee's developments is another problem. Periodic meetings of licensor and licensee provide an opportunity to evaluate the specific uses to which licensed trade secrets are being used by the licensee. A major worry for any licensor is that his licensee will not acknowledge the responsibility to disclose improvements or other inventions developed as a result of the licensed trade secrets. Grantback provisions in a license agreement are of little use unless a licensor knows about improvements. This is a particular problem when all or most of the improvements by the licensee are supposed to flow back to the licensor under a restrictive grantback provision. The longer period of time a license agreement term has to run, the less willingness there is in most licensees to hand over new improvements regardless of what the license agreement itself requires. Particularly where a licensee has a non-exclusive license and others of his competitors are licensed the same information, the resentment grows.

There is no easy answer to dealing with this prevalent licensee attitude. It is human nature to keep new improvements to yourself since the attitude is "I have already paid for this!" The best advice is to conduct frequent meetings between technical people of both licensor and licensee to exchange information. If there is a significant new development, a licensor's top technical people ought to be able to catch on and question why there has not been a specific disclosure.

Above all, a licensor wants royalties paid on time and in full. Accurate payment of royalties is made much easier by a license contract provision allowing independent audits of books and records of a licensee. This tool allows a licensor who believes there is cheating on royalties or withholding of information on new technology to proceed swiftly for an investigation without the step of prior court approval. The cost of an independent auditor is greater than allowing the internal staff of the licensor to look at the books of the licensee but use of the independent auditor tends to overcome licensee reluctance to allow an outsider to examine its books and procedures. The independent auditor is given a limited charge to look only for certain items, so the auditor need only report back to the licensor on those items which suggest a problem. This technique allows a licensee some measure of flexibility and independence, yet is legally enforceable if the licensee objects.

Conclusion

This chapter has analyzed licensing of trade secrets from the initial stage in which a company considers licensing its trade secrets through executing the agreement and transfer of trade secrets. Do not assume the stages and steps outlined in this chapter are too comprehensive for your trade secrets. There is one central approach. Clearly identify your trade secrets, decide the scope which will be licensed, and devise methods to limit their disclosure to the licensee and to any authorized third parties. At any stage in the process a misstep can mean trade secrets are irrevocably lost. In all cases there are at least three things a licensor of trade secrets must do. First, before any trade secrets are transmitted to a potential licensing partner, have the licensing partner execute a pre-disclosure secrecy agreement binding it and its key employees. Second, bind all third parties peripherally related to the licensing process with access to your trade secrets by written secrecy agreements to prevent unauthorized disclosure. And third, the formal license agreement must contain adequate protections for trade secrets during its term and allow you, as the licensor, access to new technology developed by the licensee, within reasonable limits.

7

Joint Ventures and Trade Secrets

The joint venture is an increasingly popular way to conduct business. This chapter is addressed to the company that wants to participate in a joint venture and intends to contribute its trade secrets. Practical suggestions are given for shielding trade secrets from unauthorized use at all stages of a joint venture.

What Is a Joint Venture?

The joint venture is no longer an odd duck. While it is now quite popular, few people have a clear understanding of what a joint venture actually is, how it operates, and the risks involved. Basically defined, a corporate joint venture is an agreement between two or more companies joining together to cooperate for one particular goal or project. A joint venture can be a partnership, a corporation, or other legal agreement binding together two or more parties.

How Joint Ventures Involving Trade Secrets Differ from Licensing Transactions

It is critical to appreciate the difference between a joint venture to which one party contributes trade secrets and a licensing transaction in which the trade secrets are transferred to another party.

A trade secret license transaction is normally an arms-length transaction. After the trade secret information is transmitted to the licensee, there is no continuing reason for the parties to work closely together unless there is some violation of the licensing agreement provisions. The primary concern of most licensors, therefore, is to find a responsible licensee who pays royalties in a timely fashion. Only as an afterthought do licensors seek promises not to disclose trade secrets without their authorization. Techniques for evaluation and implementation are different in a joint venture transaction from licensing.

A corporate joint venture is normally a new enterprise in which two or more companies merge resources, if only for a single project. The keys to a successful joint venture are communication and cooperation. Dealings between joint venturers are not arms length but are day-to-day and continuing. The types of risks and problems that arise for a joint venture partner who contributes trade secrets to a venture can be far greater than risks to a licensor in a licensing transaction. The problem is that in a joint venture it is difficult to limit continuing disclosures of proprietary information.

In joint ventures as in licensing, the company with trade secrets risks permanent loss of its ability to control trade secret information if it fails to protect its secrets throughout the term of the joint venture. To insure greater chances for success of a joint venture, begin a detailed analysis when the first possibility of a joint venture is raised.

This chapter will present a practical structural framework for each stage in a joint venture undertaking and will point out the trade secret pitfalls.

Eight Risks for the Trade Secret Joint Venturer

In order to simplify our analysis of joint ventures and trade secrets, we will use a hypothetical joint venture in this chapter. Two existing United States companies form a joint venture. One company is a small growing organization possessing valuable trade secrets in a high-tech area. The other company is larger and more established with strong capital resources, manufacturing, and distribution capabilities, but lacks key technological expertise. The purpose of forming the joint venture is to design, manufacture and sell throughout the United States a high-technology product based upon the existing trade secret technology of the one partner. The risks involved in the joint venture will be viewed from the perspective of the smaller company with the valuable trade secrets. How can the one maintain the integrity of its trade secrets and yet profit from them?

Any company contributing trade secrets to a joint venture faces at least eight distinct risks. Each area represents a different type of problem to be handled during negotiations or in the joint venture agreement itself. Otherwise, serious consequences are possible.

Risk #1: The Continuing Obligation to Disclose Trade Secrets

In a licensing transaction, the licensor has the luxury of deciding in advance which of its trade secrets it will transfer in exchange for royalties. This luxury does not exist for the joint venture partner with trade secrets. The nature of a joint venture is a continuing and intimate relationship between joint venture partners. The partner with the trade secrets will be expected not only to disclose trade secrets when the joint venture begins, but is urged continuously for the life of the joint venture to disclose more. Venture partners invariably attempt to obtain not only trade secrets within the scope of the joint venture, but also those beyond its scope. Close contact among partners increases disclosure possibilities with or without evil intent. The risk is clear. The venturer with trade secrets may not know what "price" is required in order to play in the game. A company should be aware of the dangers of continuous disclosure before entering into a joint venture.

Risk #2: Employees of Your Joint Venture Partner

The greatest risk to any company's trade secrets comes from its present and past employees. In a joint venture, the risks are doubled with the disclosure of trade secrets to employees of the joint venture partner. Further, the employees of the joint venture itself often have some direct loyalty to one or more of the partners. As difficult as it is to control one's own employees when it comes to trade secrets, the problem is compounded geometrically when a joint venture is undertaken. You must establish strict parameters for how employees of your joint venture partners and the joint venture handle and disseminate all aspects of trade secret information.

Risk #3: Third Parties Dealing with Joint Venture

Any joint venture will need at some point to deal with outside accountants, lawyers, bankers, consultants, subcontractors, and suppliers. Any one of them is a potential risk group. Strict conditions must be established from the beginning for dealing with outsiders to protect a joint venture's trade secrets and proprietary information. If your trade secrets are involved, you should take positive steps to ensure that the joint venture formulates procedures to protect trade secrets that are every bit as strict as exist in your own company. It is vital that controls be instituted by the joint venture partners, because the outside third parties will be dealing with the joint venture itself and not with individual companies. Outsiders have no obligation to protect your trade secrets, unless the joint venture communicates and enforces the secrecy restrictions and makes compliance the essential element for a continuing relationship.

Risk #4: The After-Developed Technologies and Trade Secrets

After a joint venture commences and one of the joint venture partners independently develops a new technology or important technical advance, you should know in advance who has rights to the after-developed technology. Unfortunately, this is an area potential joint venture partners tend to overlook during negotiations. The failure to precisely define the scope of the joint venture and the contributions made by each partner will lead to serious problems during the term of the venture. In some cases, this omission results at the end of an otherwise successful joint venture. Your joint venture agreement should define the purpose for the joint venture, specify the initial and subsequent contributions of trade secrets expected from each partner, and provide in detail what is the status of after-developed technologies by any partner. If each partner will be obligated to contribute after-developed technologies, decide in advance whether additional compensation goes to the one who makes additional contributions of trade secrets.

Risk #5: Non-Joint Venture Activities

Before entering into a joint venture, examine your potential partners closely. Do not merely consider the resources each will contribute to the joint venture. Look also at what other non-joint venture activities your potential partners do in the course of their normal business. The risk is that your trade secrets which become part of the joint venture will be appropriated by another joint venture partner and used in connection with non-joint venture activities. A control mechanism is needed to regulate how your trade secrets are used and where they may *not* be used by your joint venture partners. The joint venture agreement should specifically define whether or not trade secrets may at any time be used by joint venture partners for their non-venture activities. Again, this is an area frequently overlooked in joint venture agreements. Failure to address it results in serious problems for trade secrets owners.

Risk #6: The Expanding Scope of a Joint Venture

The scope and direction for a joint venture should be set at its initial stage. At that point each party should understand what its contributions, liabilities, and rewards ought to be. A successful and rapidly growing joint venture can quickly branch out or move into areas not initially anticipated. On an annual basis, all joint venture partners should jointly evaluate whether their joint activities are going beyond the project and goals agreed to and embodied in their joint venture agreement. Failure to reassess on a continuing basis raises the spectre of trade secrets of a joint venture partner being used in areas which either conflict with existing activities of that individual partner or impinge upon a company's ability to license or use its trade secrets in other ways. Of course, joint venture partners who have not contributed trade secrets to the venture benefit by an ever-expanding scope of the venture. The basic concept is definition of a limited scope for the venture initially and maintenance of control during the term of the agreement. Activities and trade secrets will not then expand without the unanimous agreement of all partners.

Risk #7: Creating Your Perfect Competitor

Most companies undertake joint ventures because their current resources are not adequate. Each joint venturer adds some key element to the overall transaction. Companies with valuable trade secrets or technology often seek joint venture partners because they lack the capital, distribution mechanisms, or other ancillary resources essential to fully exploit the technology. The chance to bind together with a joint venture partner with capital resources and other strengths is a strong lure to a company that wishes to avoid overextending its individual capacities. For a company long on technology but short in other areas, the joint venture appears an unbeatable combination. However, do not lose sight of the fact that once a company obtains rights to your technology and possesses capital resources, you have a potential long-term competitor. Therefore, initially analyze the long-term effects of the joint venture over the short-term benefits before deciding on its overall desirability.

Risk #8: The Price of Failure

When a license agreement terminates unexpectedly, a licensor must be prepared to minimize the damage. In a joint venture, continuing interaction between joint venture partners makes all parties intimately aware of the activities of the others. If the venture is going badly, it is difficult for the partner who has contributed trade secrets to hold back or to hide something in anticipation that the venture will fail. As a result, the impact of the failure or premature termination of the joint venture is significant. The problem is particularly acute for the joint venturer which is small and without capital resources. A failed venture can mean either a strongly financed competitor with new technology is created or a loss of the chance to penetrate new markets. This risk is particularly dangerous in fast-moving, high-tech fields.

What You Should Know About Joint Ventures and the Antitrust Laws

Before seriously exploring a joint venture opportunity, remember the existence of the United States antitrust laws. Not all joint ventures are legal under federal and state antitrust statutes. Antitrust and anticompetition laws are designed to prohibit agreements, contracts, and joint ventures that unreasonably eliminate competition in the market place. There are five basic antitrust questions to ask about any joint venture. First, will the joint venture effectively eliminate producers or products from the market place which would otherwise be competitive? Second, what share of the relevant market will the joint venture control? Third, what is the definition of the market the joint venture will be involved in? Fourth, will formal agreements be signed by the joint venture partners restricting their activities so that they will not compete directly? Fifth, by forming a joint venture are there companies which have been excluded from the joint venture who will be adversely affected? While to the non-lawyer these questions may seem unimportant, they are not. To avoid costly problems, involve an experienced lawyer with a clear understanding of antitrust laws at an early stage of the joint venture planning process.

Antitrust and Joint Ventures Intended for Research and Development

With the increasingly high costs of developing new technologies and applications, United States companies are now beginning to explore whether they should join together and pool research-related efforts. The United States Department of Justice has published a book entitled "Antitrust Guide Concerning Research Joint Ventures." The basic position advanced by the Justice Department is that joint venture activities encouraging pooled-research activities which are justifiable for business reasons probably do not violate federal antitrust laws. In late 1983, the United States Attorney General on behalf of the Department of Justice formally issued a letter approving the formation of a consortia joint venture of New England companies that wished to combine their research and development efforts to implement new technologies. The formal approval represents a significant step for the Justice Department. Prior to this, the "best" the Justice Department could do was to express no present intent of challenging activities. Assuming antitrust issues are examined in advance for a joint venture research and development operation, it can present a unique opportunity to exchange trade secrets. If all members of the joint venture contribute and share equally in the fruits of the research, trade secrets are relatively safe.

On October 12, 1984, the United States Congress passed "The National Cooperative Research Act." The Act sets up a notification procedure by which coventurers can receive protection from treble damage antitrust lawsuits. This new law is a clear sign of governmental recognition of the need to encourage R&D joint ventures. Because of limitations on who will be qualified to participate in R&D joint ventures, only time will tell if it will be widely used. Be sure to analyze carefully the benefits available under the law before entering into a research joint venture.

Antitrust and Non-Competitive Joint Ventures

In setting up joint ventures, the parties sometimes contemplate it would be better not to compete with each other in the United States in the sale of independently produced products or the supplying of services. This temptation should be strictly avoided. There is a good chance such an agreement will violate the federal antitrust laws. However, if two or more companies wanted to limit competition between themselves and their jointly owned venture, this might be acceptable as long as one of the joint venture partners is not dominant in the particular market. Again, check with a competent United States attorney before agreeing to any restriction along these lines.

Antitrust and the Joint Venture Setup to Produce a New Product

A joint venture frequently encountered is an effort to produce a new product. One venture partner contributes technology while the other contributes capital and ancillary services. Two basic United States antitrust issues must be evaluated. The first issue is whether either of the two joint venturers would have entered into the specific market if the joint venture had not existed. If a joint venture is the only means by which the two companies can enter into a particular market, there probably is no problem. A second issue is how competitive the market is, that is, how many companies are involved and their relative sizes. If a market has twenty-five hundred competitors and two small companies could have entered independently or could have joined forces as a joint venture, that joint venture should not face antitrust hurdles. Again, it is important to understand that the federal antitrust laws are designed to foster actual and potential competition within the United States.

The Influence of Foreign Antitrust Laws on a Joint Venture

Joint ventures are sometimes put together to enable two or more United States companies to compete in foreign markets. As long as the activities of the joint venture have no reasonably foreseeable, substantial impact on United States consumers or other domestic competitors, those joint ventures will not violate federal antitrust laws. The passage of the *Export Trading Company Act of 1982* helped to answer many uncertainties about these antitrust laws as they affect joint ventures operating abroad. Chapter Eight will discuss the *Export Trading Company Act* at greater length.

To the extent that a joint venture affects the markets or consumers of a country outside the United States, there can be a problem. For example, the European Economic Community (E.E.C.) has a comprehensive antitrust/anticompetition law that in some ways parallels our federal antitrust theories. If the activities of a joint venture are carried out in the European Economic Community, evaluate in advance which activities can be undertaken safely under the E.E.C. laws. Even if there are no problems with E.E.C. antitrust laws, individual countries, such as Germany, France, and England, with antitrust laws may cause you problems within their jurisdictional areas. Japan, too, has an antitrust law but it tends not to be as strictly observed as those in Europe.

The point to be stressed is not that businessmen should become antitrust experts, but that they must understand how a joint venture, if not properly structured, can lead to serious civil and possibly criminal antitrust problems.

An Overview of the Stages of a Joint Venture Transaction

To best understand how to protect trade secrets in joint ventures, start by breaking the entire process into three distinct stages. Stage One is the evaluation process that focuses on whether a joint venture is desirable for a company with trade secrets. Included are techniques for locating potential partners and the pre-negotiation agreement. Stage Two is the critical negotiation process and the pitfalls to avoid. Stage Three is the joint venture agreement itself and examines how trade secrets are handled during the joint venture term. It also suggests what action to take when the joint venture terminates, particularly if a termination occurs earlier than initially anticipated.

Stage One: How to Locate Potential Joint Venture Partners and Protect Trade Secrets by a Pre-negotiation Secrecy Agreement

A common genesis for a joint venture results when two parties have informally worked together and because of the relationship are comfortable with each other. An idea is suggested, and the joint venture is born. However, for the analysis which follows we will assume your company with its valuable trade secrets wishes to enter into a joint venture and has *not* already preselected potential venture partners. The goal is to locate the best possible partners and maximize the possibilities for success. As in all successful business operations, an overall concept and plan are essential from the beginning. The selection process must be methodical and structured if serious risks are to be avoided. Preparation of a Joint Venture Profile will assist greatly in the selection process.

The Joint Venture Profile—Goals and Scope

You must draft a joint venture profile before seeking partners. The goal and the proposed scope of the venture activities must be clearly understood in advance. Test yourself by writing two or three sentences describing the underlying purpose for the proposed venture. Inability at an initial stage to define goals precisely suggests a lack of adequate preparation.

As a general rule, a joint venture created to pursue multiple ends poses greater difficulties for the selection of partners than does a more limited undertaking. For example, a joint venture of two companies to design, develop and market an anesthesia mask for sale in the United States market is more manageable than a venture of general cooperation between a small medical high-tech company and a large medical products distributor to develop unspecified products suitable for sale in the bio-medical market over an indefinite time period.

Therefore, you should draw clear parameters around the proposed operations of a joint venture before you look for partners. This is particularly critical for a company with trade secrets that will become its part of the "bargain" in forming the joint venture.

The Joint Venture Profile: What Resources Are Required to Make the Joint Venture Work?

Once you decide upon the goals and scope of the venture, you next must define the specific resources required to make it work. Obviously, if a company possesses all the required resources, there is no need for a joint venture unless there is a need to spread the risk. If a partner is desirable, the resources required, who possesses them, and the ideal number of players are the critical issues to resolve.

There are at least four basic resources to evaluate when planning a joint venture. The relative importance of each and their relationship to each other will determine which players ultimately become part of the joint venture.

Resource #1—the importance of technology to the venture

Perhaps the key element in any joint venture involving the development, marketing and distribution of a new product or service is the technological expertise contributed by one or more of the venture partners. In many joint ventures and in our hypothetical example, the small company on the leading edge of a new technology finds itself sought after as a potential partner solely because of its unique technology in a particular field. Technology can come in the form of patents and/or trade secret information, including know-how. In most cases even patents are most valuable when used in connection with trade secrets. By possessing technology, particularly technology which is patented, a company is in a unique position to leverage itself in a joint venture far beyond its size. Conversely, the risks to the company with trade secret technology in a joint venture are frequently greater than the risks to the other partners who have made non-technology contributions.

Resource #2—the importance of financial resources to the joint venture

Valuable and innovative technologies go unexploited everyday due to the unavailability of adequate financial resources. You must estimate the amount of capital for initial and ongoing needs at the beginning of the planning process. Constant re-evaluation is mandatory. The venture partner prepared to bring money to the table will traditionally expect to exercise greater control over the venture than other partners. Although this may be unrealistic, it is reality. For this reason, any company with valuable technology must decide in advance whether or not alternate methods of obtaining capital exist. The increasing numbers of independent venture capital groups who seek a passive role in a joint venture as opposed to active participation with a guaranteed equity ownership offer one alternative place to look. Also, since the equity ownership position of venture capitalists can be reduced subsequently by the exercise of stock warrants if the venture becomes extremely successful, consider talking to established venture capitalists. Capital, then, should be the last resource to be evaluated in planning for a joint venture and evaluating the need for partners.

Resource #3—the marketing of products and services

The ability to market, distribute, and sell products or services is a crucial element in any joint venture or business. In planning a joint venture, look carefully for companies with these skills. Geographic strength and expertise in specific markets are always relevant. If a proposed partner does not now possess these skills but intends to develop them during the course of the venture, the best advice is to look elsewhere. A track record of performance, not promises or potential, should act as the criterion in selection.

Resource #4—the business reputation of potential partners

Aside from the ability to market the products or services of a joint venture, the reputations and the stature of companies within their market sector can make them desirable partners. For example, the mere announcement of the future entry of International Business Machines (IBM) into the personal computer market sent a wave of apprehension throughout the entire industry. This was based on IBM's reputation as an intensely strong and sophisticated marketer. Similarly, in joint ventures which involve construction projects or the supplying of services, long-term demonstrable experience coupled with a reputation for effectiveness can be an important asset. The point is not to underestimate the commercial value of the "right" partner.

What Is the Right Number of Partners for the Joint Venture?

After you have developed a specific Joint Venture Profile and evaluated the relative importance of the four resources common to joint ventures, the question remains—how many joint venture partners are desirable? The simplest and best advice is the fewer partners, the better. If two or three potential partners can among themselves fulfill most of the resource requirements, consider buying or contracting for any missing elements instead of looking for additional partners. The difficulties which can arise in dealing with just one partner become increasingly more difficult when two or more partners are added to the picture.

The number of joint venture partners is particularly critical to our hypothetical company which intends to contribute all or a major part of its proprietary trade secrets to the joint venture. To repeat the underlying theme of this book, the major risks to trade secrets traditionally come from individuals within an organization who can in a legitimate manner obtain access to trade secret information. Limiting the scope and degree of possible access to trade secrets is the preferable approach. Therefore, the greater the number of joint venturers and their employees, the greater the risk to trade secrets becomes.

Who Is Best Qualified to Locate Potential Joint Venture Partners?

Once the Joint Venture Profile is developed and all elements evaluated, you must decide who is best qualified to seek out the most eligible partners. In order for the partner search to work well, the right person must locate and then select, in a totally objective manner, the best candidates.

There are two basic options. Option one is to make use of existing in-house personnel to search for joint venture partners. Option two is to hire an outside consultant for the specific task. In the analysis of licensing transactions and trade secrets in Chapter Six, you were strongly encouraged to use an outside consultant. In the joint venture area, it is less clear which option is preferable.

There are three advantages to using in-house staff to find joint venture partners. First, since a joint venture requires an intimate and continuing relationship between two or more joint venture partners, it is far more important to understand all the elements and activities of a particular company for joint venture purposes than it is when seeking a licensing partner. The cost of the search is a second point to consider, since the process of forming a joint venture normally takes longer than the licensing of technology. As a result, the cost of an outside consultant in the joint venture search process can be higher than if a license were involved. The final factor is that negotiating a joint venture is an evolutionary process. Your initial Joint Venture Profile will change over time. This is less likely to happen in a licensing transaction where the License Prospectus remains fairly constant.

On the other hand, there are two advantages to using an outside consultant in seeking joint venture partners. Since the desire in a joint venture is a long-term profitable relationship, objectivity is most important. Where a corporation or potential joint venture partner uses its own employees in the venture, there exist certain allegiances or long-term relationships because of their corporate employment. These relationships limit the possibility for true objectivity in evaluating potential partners. The obvious human tendency is to prefer friends over others. Consultants are freer of bias. The second advantage of an outside consultant is the access to multiple and untraditional sources of information in finding potential joint venture partners. Frequently, the resources which only the consultant can tap are well worth the expense in the long run.

Where in-house personnel are used initially in locating joint venture partners, they should be charged with the task of finding as many potential partners as possible that fit the Joint Venture Profile. After the list is developed, consider retaining an outside consultant to review the possible candidates on an objective, quantitative basis.

How to Select the Best Joint Venture Partner—
Quantify the Joint Venture Profile

Assume you have isolated five potential joint venture partners. You must be able to evaluate their relative strengths to find the best possible partner or partners. Initiate the process by quantifying your Joint Venture Profile. This should precede any negotiations or substantive talks with potential joint venture partners. For example, if the joint venture will rely to a great extent on the contribution of trade secrets and proprietary information, give this factor a higher quantitative value. In the event capital is absolutely essential to the long-term viability of the project, the ability of a partner to invest money in the venture will receive a higher rate. A model of a quantitative profile is given in Figure Two (page 148).

Figure Two

QUANTIFIED JOINT VENTURE PROFILE

Scope: Venture to Develop and Market Anesthesia Mask in the United States

	Desired Rating	Prospect #1	Prospect #2	Prospect #3	Prospect #4	Prospect #5
Trade Secrets/ Proprietary Information	5	8	4	2	2	2
Capitalization	6	2	5	8	10	4
Domestic Distribution Capabilities	8	6	2	5	6	7
International Distribution Capabilities	5	1	2	8	6	4
Size of Company	8	6	6	5	7	4
Reputation/Experience in Medical Equipment Field	9	6	5	8	9	5
Compatibility of Management Structures	6	7	4	3	5	4
TOTALS:	47	36	28	39	45	30

1 = Minimum Rating
10 = Maximum Rating

Once each prospective joint venture partner has been quantitatively rated, ask additional questions about each one. The responses to these questions should affect their relative standing. Some possible questions to ask are:

—What is the long-term financial strength of each potential joint venture partner aside from the initial capitalization requirements?

—What is the existing management structure of the potential joint venture partners from the standpoint of continuity? Do you foresee changes in the near future?

—Does the current management structure of each potential joint venture partner tend to complement your own company's structure and operations?

—What is the size of the potential joint venture partners and are they a comfortable match with your company?

—Are the potential joint venture partners now involved in any activities or operations which might be inconsistent with the goals of the joint venture?

—What are the existing policies of potential joint venture partners on handling and protecting trade secret information? Have they ever been involved in any trade secret or patent litigation?

—Is any potential joint venture partner involved in litigation or other securities-related matters which might adversely affect its long-term viability?

—What is the general reputation in the industry of each potential joint venture partner?

—Do the long-term goals of the potential joint venture partner's company appear to go in the same general direction as the proposed joint venture?

—Are the proposed joint venture partners now involved in any other joint ventures?

—If a potential partner is involved in other joint ventures, who are the partners in those ventures and are there any possible conflicts or problems?

—Does any potential joint venture partner have any other weaknesses or problems which might affect the activities of the joint venture?

It is strongly recommended that before any negotiations begin with possible joint venture partners you hire an outside consultant to get an objective opinion of your Joint Venture Profile. Ask the consultant to evaluate your ratings of each possible partner. Once negotiations have started, the opportunity for objective comments is gone; this critical point should not be missed. Do not totally rely on in-house staff if you need unbiased evaluations.

The Pre-Negotiation Joint Venture Secrecy Agreement

If your company owns or controls proprietary information that may be useful to a joint venture, you must be particularly careful. Unless trade secrets and proprietary information are properly shielded during the negotiation stage, irreparable harm may result, particularly if the joint venture negotiations collapse and no venture emerges.

Before any discussions or negotiations begin, all parties should sign a pre-negotiation secrecy agreement. Insist that all parties sign a secrecy agreement whether or not the discussions are intended to be substantive in nature. Resist the sweet song of those companies which respond to your request that when the talks become "serious" or "substantive" they will sign an agreement binding them to secrecy. Any company with valuable trade secrets and proprietary information must be particularly wary of the danger that the a "look-now-and-sign-later" attitude reflects. Although some lawyers advise their clients that an oral promise to maintain trade secrets is enforceable in court, it is foolish, even stupid, to rely on the oral promise of a potential partner to protect your secrets. In short, insist at the beginning on the execution of a secrecy agreement or immediately terminate negotiations.

If for some reason you have already started negotiations or talks with potential partners, under no circumstance reveal any of your trade secrets or proprietary information before your negotiating partners sign a secrecy agreement. Remember, there is no such thing as a standard secrecy agreement that will be applicable in all joint negotiations. Do not rely on a form you find in a book without first checking with experienced legal counsel.

There are a minimum of six key elements in most good secrecy agreements. They are discussed below.

How to define trade secret information
in the secrecy agreement

During the course of negotiating a joint venture, you may be asked to disclose a broad range of trade secret information to other potential partners to assist them in studying the venture opportunity. The secrecy agreement must clearly define the scope of trade secret information. Obviously, any information relating to unpatented products, processes, or ideas in development is a trade secret and subject to the protection of the agreement. While these constitute the area of greatest potential exposure, in defining trade secret information do not ignore the value to your company of corporate information such as marketing plans, geographic strengths, financial and legal information, know-how as applied to possible joint venture products, processes and operations, industrial formulations, customer-related information, and specific background on your machinery and other capital equipment available for use by a joint venture. Try to encompass as much of your information as possible within the umbrella of the secrecy agreement.

Who is bound by the secrecy agreement?

To legally bind a corporation, a secrecy agreement must be signed by either an officer of the corporation or a person who is duly authorized to bind the corporation. If there is any question of someone's authority to bind the corporation, ask for verification. One approach is to request the highest possible officer in a company to sign the secrecy agreement. Why? Simply, the act of signing forces an acknowledgement, at a high executive level of your potential partner, of the significance of the secrecy contract. This tends to lessen the chances that your potential partner will minimize the nature or importance of the secrecy agreement and your trade secrets.

Particularly when you are dealing with a large company that has many employees, identify which employees of your potential partners will have actual access to your trade secrets that are transmitted as part of the joint venture negotiations. It is recommended that you provide in the secrecy agreement for advance written notice of each person employed by your potential partners who will examine your trade secrets. Obligate those employees to sign individual secrecy agreements. The point here is to impress on individual employees the true significance and importance of the trade secret information they are handling during the planning stages and negotiation phase of a potential venture. Also, consider placing an affirmative contractual obligation on your negotiating partners to advise you if and when any individuals not employed by them will have access to your trade secrets during negotiations. For example, will your partner need to show outside consultants, bankers, lawyers, or accountants your trade secrets in the course of the joint venture negotiations? If this is a possibility, demand to know in advance under what circumstances your trade secrets will be transmitted to a third party. In any case, require prior written notice before any of your secrets are shown. With prior notice, you can decide whether an individual secrecy agreement from third parties is reasonable under the particular circumstances.

Marking Documents

The pre-negotiation secrecy agreement must stipulate that any document or other corporate information considered trade secret information is clearly marked at the time it is transmitted to a potential joint venture partner. The simplest method is to make a rubber stamp or similar marking device which states something like the following:

THIS IS TRADE SECRET INFORMATION OF THE _____ COMPANY WHICH IS DISCLOSED TO _____ WHO IS LEGALLY BOUND BY A SECRECY AGREEMENT NOT TO DISCLOSE THIS DOCUMENT WITHOUT PRIOR WRITTEN AUTHORIZATION OF _____. UNAUTHORIZED DISCLOSURE BY ANY PERSON MAY RESULT IN CIVIL AND/OR CRIMINAL LIABILITY.

If a document of more than a single page is transmitted, stamp the notice on each page so it clearly appears on its face. Place the notice in such a fashion that it may not be removed or erased without being readily apparent. For example, a rubber stamp with the proper notice could be stamped in red ink in the middle of each typed page. This is particularly important since most employees have easy access to photocopying equipment, and such a notice makes it impossible to remove the notice without obliterating the page or retyping it. Also, consecutively mark every page and demand signed detailed receipts from your potential partners where appropriate.

The time period for the secrecy agreement

There are two aspects to the time element of a pre-negotiation secrecy agreement. First, give your potential partners a specific period of time in which to review and evaluate the joint venture to decide if a deal makes sense. For the company which is disclosing its key trade secrets or other proprietary information during negotiations, limit the disclosure to a maximum of 60 to 90 days. If negotiations are not completed in that period, there should be a contractual obligation on all parties to immediately return your trade secrets and other proprietary information, including copies, in their possession. If negotiations are to proceed beyond the initial defined period, require a written extension with the other party. The reason for this procedure is to impress upon your negotiating partners the importance of the trade secrets disclosed, the legal obligation to return them in a defined period, and the liabilities of wrongful disclosure.

The second aspect of "time" in a secrecy agreement involves the possibility that the negotiations will not be successful. The trade secret agreement, in addition to requiring the return of the trade secrets, must legally bind your unsuccessful joint venture partner, its employees, and any other entities to which your trade secrets were disclosed to keep it secret for some time into the future. Place a specific time period on the life of the secrecy agreement. Anything beyond ten years is probably not reasonable. Courts do not look favorably upon secrecy agreements that are to last forever.

The right to injunctive relief

If trade secret information is properly transmitted during a joint venture negotiation and is later wrongfully revealed, immediate action is required. Since once trade secrets are available to the public they are no longer legally protectable, so the need to limit their disclosure is far more important in the short run than any damages that can be recovered later in court from the guilty party. Therefore, a secrecy agreement must give your company the immediate right to seek injunctive relief in a court of its choosing. Since an injunction is an extraordinary type of court action which under certain circumstances can be quickly obtained, the right to ask a specific court for help without jurisdictional challenge is critical. Chapter Ten will present in great detail the role of the injunction in protecting trade secrets.

Damages

The secrecy agreement can act as a tool to advise your possible partners of the risks they run if they misuse your trade secrets. Besides stipulating that you have the right to seek injunctive relief if there is a wrongful disclosure, note in the agreement that you independently have the right to ask a court for damages. Some secrecy agreements include a clause called a "liquidated damages" provision. Liquidated damages is a contract provision in which, at the time the agreement is signed, the parties agree in advance how much it will cost a party who wrongfully discloses trade secrets. Since laws in the United States vary from state to state, it is necessary to consult competent legal counsel before including a liquidated damages provision in a contract. In any case, a secrecy agreement should put all parties on notice of their exposure to lawsuits if improper disclosures occur.

Stage Two: Negotiating Joint Ventures

Negotiating a joint venture is no different from negotiating any other type of contract. Assuming each party knows its own interests well, the question is whether or not the joint venture results in benefits greater than the potential risks. For the company contributing its trade secrets to a joint venture, four concerns should dominate its thinking during the negotiation process.

The most important concern for the owner of trade secrets is to restrict the amount and quality of trade secret information passed on to potential partners until it becomes a certainty that a joint venture will be consummated. Companies with trade secrets must be constantly on their guard, because their prospective partners invariably demand access to as many trade secrets as possible. The best advice is to reveal as little as possible. When a request for additional trade secrets is made by a negotiating party, evaluate whether it is vital to the negotiations or if the party appears to be on a fishing expedition.

The second concern is to follow a strict time limit for negotiations. Once the basic pre-disclosure secrecy agreement is signed, set a period of 30, 60 or 90 days for definable progress to be made or else the negotiations are at an end. The company with trade secrets is the one at greatest risk the longer its secrets are outside its immediate control. If negotiations stretch on beyond three months, trade secrets are invariably assimilated by the potential joint venture partners. Therefore, the shorter the negotiation process, the less risk of loss to your valuable proprietary information.

The next point to remember in negotiations is to establish a procedure for continually identifying those specific employees of your potential partners who will have access to proprietary information. At the beginning of negotiations, designate a specific employee of each potential joint venture partner through whom all communications are directed. Request on a periodic basis during the negotiations the names, titles, and activities of those new employees of your negotiating partners. Insist upon individual secrecy agreements for those who pose the greatest potential risk to you if your secrets are wrongfully appropriated. Be particularly cautious when dealing with a subsidiary or division of a large company. Stipulate that during negotiations proprietary information disclosed to a particular subsidiary or division of a company will not be disclosed without prior written authorization to any other part of that company or related entity.

A final consideration is that your potential partners may want to show their lawyers, accontants, consultants, suppliers, or bankers information about items revealed during the negotiations. Propose a general agreement that no trade secrets are to be shown to any outside party without prior written notice to all. It is strongly recommended that when permission is given for outsiders to examine your proprietary information you insist on individual secrecy agreements signed by the outsiders. Only a written document which threatens serious legal liability will force third parties to place the proper emphasis on the extent of their obligation to shield the trade secrets of others.

What to Do If Joint Venture Negotiations Collapse

When negotiations reach a successful conclusion, everyone is happy. Unfortunately, many negotiations frequently fall apart. If this happens, an important consideration is whether any or all of the parties anticipate or desire an ongoing relationship aside from a joint venture at some point in the future. It is more likely in a joint venture negotiation, as opposed to a licensing transaction, that the parties will have some contact at a later point. Since joint ventures are often formed on the basis of a pre-existing customer or supplier relationship between parties, good sense and sensitivity to the possible pitfalls of the situation need to be examined closely. Depending upon the desire for future relationships, the suggestions as to termination which follow may have to be adjusted accordingly. As a general rule, it is better to err on the side of strict and formalized cessation of negotiations rather than allow matters to remain in limbo.

The Five Steps to Follow when Terminating
Joint Venture Negotiations

Joint venture negotiations can fail for any number of reasons. The number of parties, the complexity of the negotiations, or the length of negotiations can trigger the inability to reach an agreement.

Be prepared to act quickly when it is clear the party's over. There are five key steps any company with its own trade secrets at risk should follow when venture negotiations fall apart.

Step 1—formal termination of joint venture negotiations

Your first step is to send formal written notification to your negotiating partners stating that negotiations are at an end. Draft the termination letter in clear, non-legal language. Direct the letter to the lead persons negotiating for their principals. Send copies to all other members of the negotiating team so that they know the talks are concluded. It is not necessary to detail the reasons for the failure of the negotiations in your letter.

When termination letters are sent outside the boundaries of the United States or to a location where mail delivery is not always reliable, confirm the mailing with a Telex, cable, or electronic mail transfer, so that there is no question that all parties are notified. If more than one division or subsidiary of a larger company has been involved during the negotiating process, forward notices to each. If your negotiating partners maintain an in-house legal staff or outside legal advisors, make sure they all get a copy.

Step 2—the notification of key individuals.

Hopefully, prior to entering into substantive negotiations, all key individuals of the negotiating parties have signed secrecy agreements binding them to keep trade secret information protected from disclosure. At the same time formal notification goes to each joint venture partner confirming that negotiations are finished, each individual who has signed a secrecy agreement should be notified. This is only possible if throughout the course of negotiations you have accurately tracked those individuals who have signed secrecy agreements. It is important to know in advance specific office locations of the employees. The purpose of the individual notice is to emphasize the fact that the individual may be personally civilly and/or criminally liable if he wrongfully discloses trade secrets. The notice reminds employees that their access to your trade secrets was solely for the purpose of evaluating the joint venture. Notices signed by a General Counsel or outside lawyers tend to receive the most serious consideration.

Step 3—the protection of trade secret documents

As part of the original termination letter or by separate document, notify your negotiating partners to return *all* trade secret documents and information immediately. This includes the return of all copies of documents or information. Where information is inputted on electronic storage, it is to be erased and written confirmation of this should be sent to top officials of your negotiating partners. Include in your demand a statement that failure to comply may result in civil and/or criminal penalties. That will get their attention. Of course, if an ongoing relationship with any party is anticipated, the form and degree of the demand may have to be tempered. If all the pages of all documents have been consecutively marked at the time they are turned over during negotiations, it is relatively simple to check if at least one complete set of all documents is returned later.

Try to find out whether there were several depositories where trade secret information was kept. Pass along copies of the notification letter to a responsible person at all possible depository locations, demanding return of your trade secret documents.

Set a specific time limit for the return of your documents. Put this time demand in the letter. For example, state that "within fourteen days from the date of receipt of this letter all trade secret documents of   (your company)   are to be accumulated and forwarded to (a specific person) ." Provide a contact phone number in your notice letter so that answers to any questions or problems which arise concerning the return of documents are dealt with quickly.

Step 4—formal notices to third parties

During joint venture negotiations, the advice of outsiders is often requested. Where an outside lawyer, accountant, banker, and/or consultant have access to your trade secret information, as stated earlier they should sign individual secrecy agreements. While most third parties are generally reluctant to sign any kind of secrecy agreement, follow one simple rule—"no secrecy agreement, no disclosure." However, even if you are unable to have outsiders sign a secrecy agreement, keep an accurate list of all those who have had access to your trade secret information. Then, regardless of who executed a secrecy contract, give all outsiders at the termination of the negotiations a written notice to return all trade secret information and copies in their possession. The legal reason for putting third parties on formal notice is that they have to be made aware that if they permit the illegal dissemination of trade secrets they will be liable for damages. Experienced third parties will understand the possibility of becoming defendants in future lawsuits, so the notice itself may be enough.

Step 5—keeping tabs on the future activities of your former negotiating partners

After joint venture negotiations have collapsed or been amicably terminated, it is a good idea to keep close tabs for at least one year on the future activities of former negotiating partners. Watch to see if they have entered into the production of new products or have become involved in activities that may be a part of your trade secret information received during the negotiations. A second factor to consider is whether a former negotiating partner has recently entered into joint ventures or transactions with your potential competitors. Ask if the trade secrets obtained in your negotiations have been revealed to them. Finally, if at all possible, check out former key employees of your negotiating partners who have left and started their own businesses.

Stage Three: The Keypoints of the Joint Venture Agreement and the Operation of the Venture

The best joint venture agreements are specifically tailored to meet the needs of the joint venture partners. Length of the agreement is immaterial. In the event of a misunderstanding or if a dispute arises, the joint venture documents should act as a road map to facilitate, not complicate, amicable resolutions of problems. Particularly for the company which contributes trade secrets to a joint venture, there are a number of critical areas that must be settled in negotiations before documents are signed.

Who Will "Control" the Joint Venture?

The primary motivation for most companies entering joint ventures is the opportunity to limit exposure to risks and at the same time maximize profits. While a company with trade secrets at stake will certainly be motivated by financial factors, the more vital the trade secrets are, the more important the issue of control of the joint venture becomes. No other issue should be quite as important to the trade secret owner as the control issue. This is particularly true for a smaller company whose major contribution to a joint venture is its technology.

The problem facing companies with trade secrets is how to prevent improper dissemination of those trade secrets by joint venture partners. There are at least three areas of concern. First, who will have the power to oversee and to enforce procedures for controlling trade secrets during the joint venture? Second, who will decide when and in what manner third parties receive access to the trade secret information? Third, what happens when a joint venture ends prematurely and trade secrets are involved?

To understand how a joint venture can deal with the "control" issue, it is important to decide how many joint venture partners there will be. While the relationship between two companies under most circumstances is manageable, the addition of a third or fourth venture partner makes the process immensely more difficult. Where trade secrets are involved and there are more than two joint venture partners, the joint venture agreement must be very specific.

Regardless of the number of joint venture partners and their relative equity positions in the joint venture, the company with its trade secrets at risk must insist upon the sole right to direct compliance with trade secret procedures. Where trade secret protection procedures are ignored, the partner whose trade secrets are threatened must negotiate for the right to void the venture unilaterally. For example, if a small high-tech company is a partner in a joint venture to produce computer modems, it should insist on including a provision in the joint venture agreement granting it the unilateral power to decide how its trade secrets are to be protected by all venture parties.

The Importance of Defining Trade Secrets in a Joint Venture Agreement

If your company is concerned about its trade secrets in a joint venture, pay close attention to the definition of trade secrets and proprietary information in the joint venture agreement. Look to the extent disclosures are required. A clear understanding of trade secrets at this point is more important than in the pre-negotiation secrecy agreement, because the negotiations are over and a comprehensive disclosure of trade secrets is inevitable.

First, you should assess what the real value of trade secrets is to the specific joint venture. Consider whether the joint venture will conduct research to develop a new product, engage in manufacturing, or whether two or more venture partners are sharing different resources for a goal none could accomplish alone. Evaluate how trade secrets fit into the scheme. For the success of some joint ventures, trade secrets are crucial, while for other ventures, trade secrets play a lesser role. When their relative importance is understood, it is easier to define them.

In a small, non-complex joint venture, a brief definition may be sufficient. Generally, it is better to break down trade secrets and proprietary information into various categories. This is most helpful where disclosure of trade secrets will be extensive. Categorizing trade secrets helps to make sure the potentially most valuable trade secrets receive proper attention. If joint venturers contemplate continuous use of trade secrets, one approach is to append examples of the categories of trade secrets to the joint venture agreement. Then, if during the course of the joint venture a question comes up as to whether something ought to be treated as a trade secret, examples in the joint venture agreement can resolve the question. If your company will contribute trade secrets to the joint venture operations, be the first to advance your definition of trade secrets with illustrative examples at the time the agreement is negotiated. If the agreement is unclear, expect a court to rule against your position as one seeking to shield trade secrets.

The Scope of Trade Secret Use by the Joint Venture

The joint venture agreement must define the purpose of the joint venture if it hopes to act as a useful tool for the parties. It makes a difference whether the joint venture is designed solely as a research effort to develop new products and processes or is a manufacturing activity that will make infrequent use of trade secrets. Unfortunately, joint venture agreements often are silent about how trade secrets will be used by the venture.

An important consideration is whether there is a single initial disclosure or there is an ongoing obligation to provide trade secrets to the joint venture. Especially for the companies with trade secrets, the scope of present and future disclosures is a bothersome problem. Failure to define the scope and frequency of disclosures is bound to result in misunderstandings. Look to the anticipated life of the joint venture when evaluating the scope of trade secret disclosure. For the joint venture created solely for the limited purpose of conducting research to develop a single product, the end is always in sight. At the opposite end of the spectrum, an ongoing co-production venture to manufacture a line of products will probably require continuing disclosures of trade secrets for an indefinite period of time.

Whether the scope of the joint venture is limited or broad-based, do not overlook the legal structure of your joint venture partners. For example, where one joint venturer is the wholly owned subsidiary of a larger corporation, the joint venture agreement should require that trade secrets are to be used only by your partner and may not be revealed to a parent company or other operating divisions. Besides the safety factor for trade secrets, this gives a trade secrets owner the possibility to bargain later for disclosure in exchange for additional compensation.

Important Mechanisms for Handling Trade Secrets to Include in Your Joint Venture Agreement

There is no set of procedures or control mechanisms which will guarantee the sanctity of secrets in all cases. Each joint venture has to decide on a specific approach based upon the nature of the trade secrets involved, the number of joint venture partners, and the scope of the anticipated joint venture activities. A clear understanding which is written down as to how trade secrets will be handled by joint venture partners is vital. Any ambiguity or omission will hurt the joint venture partner with trade secrets the most. Therefore, as a company with trade secrets, insist upon defining procedures, approaches, and techniques within the joint venture agreement. Do not leave the "details for later" as your partners may urge you. Consider the following approaches when finalizing the joint venture structure.

Who will have access to trade secrets during the joint venture?

It is always a bad idea to allow all the employees of a joint venture entity or all employees of your joint venture partners to have easy access to your trade secrets. The looser the controls, the greater the chance problems will arise later. The goal is to limit those individuals within the joint venture who will be authorized to work with trade secrets. While no joint venture agreement can list every specific individual who will under all conceivable circumstances have access to trade secrets, the joint venture agreement can describe the types of employees who may legitimately work with trade secrets. In a joint venture intended to research a new product, engineers and research personnel logically need to work with technical manuals and data which are trade secrets. After identifying the eligible potential groups, one good technique successfully used by some venturers is to designate a particular person within the joint venture company who is charged with the responsibility for authorizing those who may use trade secrets. This creates a chain of responsibility that can be traced back to a single person in the event there is a problem. Think of the individual as a one-way filter. Placing the responsibility on a single individual also creates an awareness of the importance of trade secrets among those who must obtain prior permission before working with trade secrets.

Who in a joint venture should sign individual secrecy agreements?

Once the decision is made on how to designate which individual employees can receive the right to work with trade secrets, the next step is to evaluate when individual employee secrecy agreements are necessary. Assume that trade secrets have been broken down into the three levels of confidentiality and commercial value suggested in earlier chapters. This categorization in itself can be a method for requiring employees to sign secrecy agreements. For the most confidential trade secrets, the joint venture policy can state that none of those secrets will be disclosed without specific authorization and before the individual employee signs a secrecy agreement.

The secrecy agreement serves two functions. First it legally binds the employee to secrecy. And second, signing an agreement stresses to the employee the importance of the trade secrets being conveyed. Employees need to be constantly reminded. Practically speaking, unless the joint venture is extremely small, it is impractical to have *all* employees sign secrecy agreements. The indiscriminate use of secrecy agreements can diminish their psychological impact. Therefore, selectivity in application is a better approach than blanket requirements as long as it is coupled with tight controls over access to information.

The location of depositories for joint venture trade secrets and marking trade secret documents

The physical location of where trade secrets are kept is always important. In joint ventures, the possibility of more than one depository for trade secrets is not unusual. During negotiations decide which depositories are authorized for retaining the trade secret documents and then note this in the joint venture agreement. State that if there are to be additional future locations for joint trade secrets all joint venture partners must first agree. This acts as another "screen" to limit indiscriminate trade secret dissemination.

As suggested earlier, set forth a uniform marking procedure for trade secret documents and other tangible proprietary information in the final joint venture documents. Although it is not always possible to consecutively number specific documents and their pages, require in each instance that documents are appropriately marked on their face so that employees will know what documents are secret and proprietary. Employees, particularly those of joint venture partners not used to trade secret procedures, must be constantly reminded of the need for confidentiality. In short, the fact that a document is a trade secret must be clearly obvious on its face. This is critical today when photocopying machines are more accessible than water coolers in most business environments.

Word processing and computerized storage of trade secret information

Since trade secret information in the form of documents, correspondence, calculations, and other data is routinely incorporated and transmitted on machines, a serious problem exists. There is no easy solution. Where your trade secret information is inputted into a computer or word processing format, appropriate internal systems are essential, so when a request is made for the information, access is either automatically limited to those with authorization or, at a minimum, a "legend" is produced on the screen. The following is an example of what may precede and follow sensitive trade secret data:

THIS IS TRADE SECRET INFORMATION OF THE _____ _____ JOINT VENTURE. ONLY AUTHORIZED PERSONS ARE PERMITTED TO REVIEW THE FOLLOWING INFORMATION. THIS DOCUMENT IS PROTECTED BY A SECRECY AGREEMENT AND ITS IMPROPER USE OR DISSEMINATION BY UNAUTHORIZED PERSONS MAY RESULT IN CIVIL AND/OR CRIMINAL PENALTIES. UNAUTHORIZED PERSONS SHOULD IMMEDIATELY DISCONTINUE THIS REQUEST. IF YOU HAVE ANY QUESTIONS ABOUT YOUR AUTHORIZATION, CONTACT ___(Name)___ AT __(Telephone Number)__ .

Experienced computer and word-processing consultants can offer good suggestions tailored to your specific needs. Once the joint venture agreement is executed, if not before, limited access to data banks containing key trade secrets must be implemented.

The need to educate employees on trade secrets policies

If trade secrets are to be shielded from disclosure in the long-run, employees of the joint venture entity and individual joint venture companies have to be made aware of the importance of trade secrets during employment. In hiring procedures, this should be factored in. It is even more important when employees are terminated. This means a continuing employee trade secret educational program is a must. Although the joint venture document need not outline all details of a trade secret education program, agree to a concrete approach among venture partners before the venture actually begins. A good idea is to designate one person at the conclusion of negotiations who immediately implements procedures on a joint venture-wide basis to secure the trade secrets of all venture partners.

Providing for an outside audit of joint venture trade secret procedures

After a joint venture has been in operation for a period of time, your methods to protect trade secrets should operate smoothly. Insist that the joint venture agreement contain a provision requiring an outside audit (study) of the existing procedures for handling trade secrets at some point after the venture has started. This study can examine both the joint venture itself and the individual joint venture partners. If the original trade secret procedures are not being followed or are inadequate, the pressure to force greater compliance is easier to accept if it comes from an outside, impartial third party. Retain a consultant, a lawyer, a public accountant, or trade secret expert to perform the audit. Unless there are real problems, the cost will be minimal and borne equally by all venture partners.

Joint venture trade secrets and dealing with outside parties

The danger of unauthorized dissemination of a joint venture's trade secrets increases greatly when access to them is made available to unrelated outside third parties. Basic questions have to be decided before the joint venture agreement is finalized:

— What third parties legitimately need access to the trade secrets of the joint venture during its term?
— What is the procedure for approving which third parties get access to joint venture trade secrets?
— Should there be specific circumstances required before trade secrets are revealed to third parties?
— Should third parties be forced to execute secrecy agreements before examining joint venture trade secrets? Will individual employee (third-party) secrecy agreements be required?
— Who will assume responsibility for coordinating the return of trade secret information from third parties?
— What legal resources will be used against third parties who improperly handle joint venture trade secrets?

Resolve the answers to these questions before the joint venture agreement is signed. Specific suggestions were given earlier in this chapter.

The need for a legal action plan to protect joint venture trade secrets

In the event of an unauthorized disclosure of trade secrets by either an employee of the joint venture or an outside third party, immediate action is mandatory to limit whatever damage has occurred. Include in the joint venture agreement a joint cooperation statement of the venture partners. This commits the partners to a unified approach. Develop a legal action plan to ensure coordinated and aggressive prosecution of any individuals who violate the venture's trade secrets. An extensive discussion of the legal action plan appears in Chapter 10.

What to Do About New Technologies and Trade Secrets Developed During the Operation of the Joint Venture

Joint venture agreements too often fail to address an area of particular importance to all joint venture partners. Once the joint venture begins its activities and new technologies or trade secrets are developed, a question arises—To whom do the newly developed information and the unexpected fruits of the venture belong? There are two situations that commonly arise.

In one situation, the joint venture develops an improvement on a technology which was originally contributed to the joint venture by one partner. Assume that without the initial contribution of those trade secrets no subsequent improvement on that technology would be possible. Several basic questions have to be resolved before the venture begins:

—Should the joint venture have exclusive rights to any technologies or trade secrets it develops during the course of the venture even if they are an improvement or offshoot of an original contribution by one joint venture partner?

—Should the joint venture's exclusive rights to own technological improvements it develops be limited to the stated scope of the joint venture activities? What is the improvement outside the scope of the venture?

—In the case where the joint venture improvement or development adds genuine value to the initial technology, should the joint venture partner which contributed those trade secrets have residual rights or receive a royalty if this becomes a highly profitable development?

—Should the profitability to the joint venture of its technological improvement play any factor in whether a joint venture partner maintains residual rights?

—Should any or all joint venture partners receive options for those uses of the new improvements which are outside the scope of the joint venture?

Obviously, there is no right or wrong approach to these difficult policy issues. However, about one thing there is no debate. If the questions are not resolved before a joint venture agreement is executed, in all likelihood subsequent technological improvements by the venture will belong to the venture *only.* Therefore, if you are the partner making the initial trade secret contributions and you want to retain residual rights, put it in the joint venture agreement.

In the other scenario, the joint venture develops an entirely new technology which is *not* an improvement on trade secrets previously contributed. The problem here is different. What kind of formula should be established among the joint venture partners to decide how new technologies are to be handled? Assuming the technology is joint venture property, will the ownership of the technology be measured by equity interest in the joint venture, by voting control, or by some other set of criteria? Who will be able to decide whether or not the new technology should be patented or is better kept as a trade secret? The issue of "control" of the joint venture most certainly raises its ugly head when the improvements have genuine financial possibilities.

Finally, where the new technology developed by the joint venture goes beyond the scope initially anticipated by the joint venture, give thought to whether the technology will be made available to the individual joint venture partners as well as the venture. The situation becomes even more complicated when this new technology, although not within the scope of the joint venture, is interesting to the parent company or another division of a joint venture partner. Unless the joint venture agreement specifically prohibits it, you can be certain the information will, properly or improperly, be passed along to related parties outside the joint venture.

Issues to Resolve About the Termination of Joint Ventures

When a joint venture terminates, all assets including trade secrets and proprietary information are distributed among the partners. Where the termination is planned, there is no major reason for concern. The parties hopefully will divide amicably. The real problem arises when there is a premature termination not originally anticipated by the joint venture partners.

The problems in a premature termination of a joint venture

The premature termination of a joint venture may occur for any number of factors:

—A joint venture partner or its employees misappropriates trade secrets;
—A joint venture partner becomes bankrupt or insolvent;
—A dispute arises among the joint venture partners over the operation or purposes of the joint venture; or
—A joint venture partner is bought out by another company which is not interested in or is incompatible with the joint venture.

When unforeseen circumstances result in the premature termination of a joint venture, trade secrets and proprietary information are at serious risk.

When you contribute trade secrets to the joint venture, demand, if at all possible, an option to buy out your joint venture partners in the event of a premature termination. This is advisable even if the buy-out represents only a short-term solution. The key is to guarantee a length of time in order to secure control over your trade secrets and other assets of the joint venture. If your partners grant you the option, provide yourself with an adequate period of time in which to finalize the buy-out—a minimum of 90 days from the time of notice. Ninety days should be enough to secure commitments for any financing required. Negotiate for the right to bring in *any* new partners to finance the buy-out and insist on no veto power for your remaining joint venture partners. Since the valuation of joint ventures is difficult under any circumstance, consider including in the joint venture agreement a formula or an impartial procedure for setting the buy-out price of the joint venture.

Do not ignore the name of the joint venture. If goodwill is built up by the joint venture over the term of its existence, negotiate for a contractual right to operate your buy-out vehicle under the original name even if one or more of the original partners is no longer part of the joint venture.

Considerations for the Planned Termination of a Joint Venture

Where the joint venture comes to a normal end, the problems are far less complex. Be sure the joint venture contract deals with the following issues:

—Does the party to the joint venture who initially contributed trade secret information have exclusive rights to that information at the termination of the joint venture?

—Do any restrictions exist on use of trade secrets of the joint venture among the partners after its conclusion?

—What are the rights of the parties to technology which was developed independently during the joint venture?

—Are there any covenants not to compete or other restrictions still in effect for some time in the future?

—What happens to patents, copyrights, or trademarks which were developed and owned by the joint venture during its life? Who owns them?

Conclusion

Joint ventures can work. Trade secrets can be protected. The trick is to do adequate planning in advance so that your company properly shields trade secrets throughout the joint venture process, even if there is a premature termination.

8

Trade Secret Problems with International Contracts and Operations

Many successful United States companies fail miserably in international transactions because they try to apply domestic experiences to foreign activities. This chapter shows how trade secrets are viewed and treated differently throughout the world. General overviews of the European Economic Community, Japan and Latin American countries are presented to illustrate the differences. United States export control laws and antitrust statutes, as domestic bars to the use of trade secrets in international markets, are also analyzed.

The Perspective of the United States Businessman on Trade Secrets

Before examining a broad overview of how trade secrets are treated in the international arena, a review of trade secrets and their role in commerce within the United States is appropriate. Although each state has independently developed its own unique set of court decisions and legislation on trade secrets, there is, nevertheless, some degree of uniformity in the United States on many trade secret legal issues. Due to the common approach among states, it has been possible in this book to present an analysis of trade secrets that is applicable to most areas of the United States.

Trade secrets are useless unless they can be legally protected from misuse. In the United States, the courts are an invaluable tool for the owner of trade secrets. Courts will enforce reasonable trade secret contractual obligations and issue injunctions against those who mishandle trade secrets. The availability of impartial legal tribunals in the United States is an invaluable tool to the company with trade secrets. Because of the relative predictability of United States trade secret law and the ability to enforce secrecy covenants throughout this country, companies with proper planning can shield trade secrets from competitors and the general public.

Even companies with extensive experience in handling trade secrets within the United States must not make the critical error of assuming this experience qualifies them in any way to handle international contracts involving trade secrets. The rules of the game and the risks are different and constantly changing outside the United States. To survive, a clear understanding of how foreign laws and courts approach trade secrets is paramount.

Trap for the Unwary—Trade Secrets in the International Arena

To repeat, the cardinal rule for American companies is never to attempt to apply United States experiences with trade secrets to international operations or contracts. Ignoring this rule often is disastrous. There are three basic circumstances in which your company may decide to involve its trade secrets outside the United States: operating a wholly owned subsidiary, licensing of technology, or taking part in a joint venture.

Trade Secrets and the Wholly Owned Foreign Subsidiary

For the United States company with an established wholly owned facility outside the United States, problems arise involving trade secrets that would not exist if those foreign operations were in this country. One major difference lies with the foreign employees. Foreign employees of a subsidiary operate under a different set of governmental rules than their American counterparts. Since foreign employees, in order to carry out their functions, may require access to trade secrets of the United States parent company, the parent may expect to place the same legal restrictions on trade secrets over foreign employees in the foreign subsidiary as it would on employees in this country. The same degree of legal control is not possible. Specific examples of foreign laws and how they treat employees follow later in this chapter.

Licensing of Trade Secrets Outside the United States

Licensing is one of the most common methods of trade secret usage internationally. Aside from our own barriers to foreign licensing, many countries throughout the world have legislated strict impediments to transfers of technology and trade secrets within their borders. It is not unusual for foreign laws to require prior governmental approval of key terms of a license such as royalties, grantbacks of technology, and the length of the term. Approval is often needed before the license is deemed legal and enforceable in that country. These governmental restrictions combined with local courts that favor the citizens over a United States licensor are hazardous to trade secrets.

Joint Ventures and Trade Secrets in International Markets

Joint ventures comprise a third avenue for international transactions. Due to growing world markets and the speed at which new technologies are being developed, trade secrets are an integral part of many joint ventures. Unfortunately, foreign laws reflecting underlying public policies in many countries are a problem for owners of trade secrets. Although not insurmountable, foreign barriers to protecting trade secrets as part of a joint venture are a reality.

How the United States Export Control Laws Limit the Licensing, Sale, and Use of Trade Secrets Outside the United States

The Congress has made a policy decision that for national security purposes and other national policy reasons the federal government is to formally monitor the export of goods, services, and technologies produced in the United States. The statute is referred to as the Export Control Law. The law is updated periodically by the Congress and there are extensive federal regulations interpreting the law. Most United States companies recognize that our export control laws limit the sale of goods and commodities in the export market. What is far less understood is that the export control laws also limit the sale, licensing, and use of United States trade secrets internationally.

What Types of Information Are Subject to United States Export Controls?

The Department of Commerce is responsible for issuing extensive regulations which supplement the statute. One part of the regulations deals specifically with technical data and the limitations on exporting it. Technical data is defined as information of any kind that can be used, or adapted for use in the design, production, manufacture, utilization, or reconstruction of articles or materials. Data can come in any type of tangible form such as a model, blueprint, photograph, or an operating manual. Technical data can also be in intangible form such as oral advice or consultations. As a general rule, as soon as something is published and available to the general public there are few, if any, restrictions in exporting the technology or using it overseas. However, as soon as you take steps to protect your technical data from public dissemination, it is subject to review by the export control regulations. There is no high-tech/low-tech distinction. Almost anything you consider to be a trade secret or proprietary is covered. The fact that similar technical data is available in a foreign country is not necessarily a factor the federal government will accept as a justification for its use overseas. The areas of greatest interest are sources of information which have anything to do with nuclear energy, have possible military applications, or are used in the design, production or operation of aircraft. For example, a CAD/CAM system for designing products is severely restricted under the export control laws because a CAD/CAM system has potential military applications.

Do not make the mistake of assuming that if technical data is available in a public library that it is not protected by the federal export control laws. For example, if your company over a long period of time has culled and collected information relating to a particular process and all the information is drawn from public sources, this may nevertheless be restricted by United States law if you wish to use or license the information overseas. Why is this so? Since probably 95 percent of all writing is unimportant or irrelevant, the fact that your company has gone through a selection process to isolate only that information which is most relevant and helpful may make it subject to controls.

How the United States Export Control Laws Work

If your company possesses information that is technical data or information subject to our export control laws, you look first to the foreign country where the information is to go. It is much easier to export information out of the United States to a free-world country than to a Communist country or a country politically at odds with this one. Today, any exports to Cuba are strictly prohibited without prior written authorization of the government, although very few types of technology are not exportable to Canada and to member nations of the European Economic Community. After the Export Control Officers look at the country where information will be located and used, they next evaluate the uses for which it is intended and estimate what chances there are it will be re-exported to another country.

When the federal export control regulations designate restrictions on specific technical information or the country where it will be used, you must file an application with the Department of Commerce for a validated export license. The application details exactly what technical information will be sold or used overseas and specifically who will have access to it. A decision is then made whether to grant a validated export license. Your company must *not* ignore the law. The statute and regulations contain severe civil and criminal penalties for violations. Ignorance of its provisions is no excuse.

Six Points of Practical Advice to Remember About the United States Export Control Laws

Point One. Evaluate in advance whether or not your trade secrets, if used outside the United States, may require a validated export license. In the event your company has trade secrets in a number of areas, this pre-evaluation process will be helpful, so your employees will know how to take proper precautions to prevent unknowing disclosure and thus avoid corporate liability.

Point Two. If your company is approached by a foreign company asking for a license of your technology, carefully review your technology to establish if a validated export license is needed. Do this evaluation prior to disclosure of any of your trade secrets during negotiations. Also, check out the background of the potential foreign licensee or joint venture partner. If it appears the foreign company is owned by another entity that could use the technical information or if disclosure to others is possible, you may have a problem. Foreign intelligence services routinely use foreign companies as fronts and conduits to obtain key United States technology. Be very cautious.

Point Three. If anyone offers to purchase your technology, even if it is a United States company, make sure this company is not a straw party for a foreign buyer seeking your technology. If your company knowingly sells its trade secrets and technology to a United States company with the idea it will go outside the United States, you may be liable.

Point Four. Watch out for visitors to your technical facilities and plants. While most companies will give foreign visitors a view of their plants, if the visitors are from a Communist or other centrally controlled economy, it may be necessary to receive a validated export license *prior* to any disclosure even if it is in the United States.

Point Five. Watch out about hiring foreign technical personnel to work in your plant who will have access to your trade secrets. This is why you must know in advance whether the technology and trade secrets your company possesses are subject to a validated export license. For example, if you hire an engineer from India to work in the United States with your technology that may have nuclear applications, you probably need a validated export license for that foreign employee. The reason is that India is not a signatory of the Nuclear Non-Proliferation Treaty.

Point Six. If a United States company has a wholly owned subsidiary outside the United States, do not assume that under our export control laws you can automatically transmit your technology or trade secrets to your wholly owned subsidiary or division. Depending on what type of information it is and the country where it will be located, a validated export license may, nevertheless, be required.

Trade Secrets in the Common Law Countries

To conduct business internationally, United States businessmen must understand there are two basic legal systems in the non-Communist world—common law jurisdictions and civil code jurisdictions. The United States, Canada, the United Kingdom, and Australia are the primary examples of common law countries. With some exceptions, the remainder of non-Communist nations are known as the civil code (civil law) jurisdictions. The treatment of trade secrets, proprietary information, and know-how differs significantly in each system.

Common law countries adhere to a similar philosophy in solving legal problems. Under the common law, a dispute between two parties is resolved by having a judge or jury look at the facts of a case and render a decision. When the court writes an opinion on the facts in a case, the court's written opinion becomes a legal precedent. Other courts are expected to follow the decision when confronted with similar situations. This is known as the doctrine of "stare decisis." Obviously, common law countries also have statutes written by legislative bodies, but the common law philosophy that court-made decisions constitute the legal basis of the law is the central focus.

To decide whether or not something is "legal" in a common law country, lawyers study the court decisions of various jurisdictions to discern the prevalent view. Then, the lawyers make an educated guess to determine if their client's conduct is permissible. While in common law countries there is no single definition of the legal concept of trade secrets, trade secrets do have a place and meaning within the framework of court decisions. The philosophical approach in civil law countries is totally different.

Civil Law Countries and Trade Secrets

Most countries of the world are civil law jurisdictions. They are different from the common law system of the United States which most United States businesses intuitively understand. Civil law countries include most of Western Europe (except the United Kingdom), most of Central and South America, Japan, and major parts of the Far East and Africa. The approach of civil law countries is to appoint a legislative body to write and preserve all the country's laws in massive compendiums of laws called "Codes." There are generally civil codes, criminal codes, and business codes. In theory, anyone with a question can go to the appropriate code and discover what is or is not permissible without the need of a lawyer.

Lawyers are used much less often in civil law countries than in the United States. Businessmen in code countries routinely look to the appropriate commercial code to answer routine commercial questions without consulting a lawyer. Contracts in civil law jurisdictions tend to be much shorter than contracts written in common law countries. Since the commercial codes in civil law countries specifically address common issues such as termination of contracts, resolution of disputes, and accepted methods for payment, it is not necessary in those countries to include extensive descriptions of these points in written contracts used there. Reference to the civil code is all that is needed. Civil law countries experience less litigation than exists in the United States. At least one reason is that in civil law countries the code acts as a guide, while in the United States one court decision may or may not act as a precedent for another court. Only where the civil code is silent or unclear in a foreign jurisdiction are their courts asked to take an active role.

What relevance do these general observations have for the use of trade secrets in civil law countries? The surprising fact is that most civil law countries do not provide in their codes for the same degree of protection for trade secrets that exists in the United States. Some civil law countries do not mention trade secrets in their civil codes. The result is obvious. Enforcement against those who misuse trade secrets is most difficult. In the more developed civil code jurisdictions, trade secrets are included in a civil code. However, some civil codes make odd distinctions between types of corporate proprietary information. Protection, when available, is often inconsistent. For example, the French Civil Code breaks trade secrets into two distinct categories. One, the "secret de fabrique," is protected by the French Civil Code, while the "secret de commerce" is not covered. For a "secret de commerce" one must resort to limited French case law which is confusing and makes planning quite tricky.

The key point to remember is that most of the world, even those nations United States businesses perceive as highly developed, operates under civil code systems whose concepts and treatment of trade secrets differ radically from those used in the United States. Careful attention must be given to any involvement in a civil code country where trade secrets are part of a joint venture, license, or business activity. Even if contractual obligations exist between a United States parent and its wholly owned subsidiary in a civil code country, the law of that foreign country may make it difficult or impossible to enforce contractual trade secret restrictions in that country. This is true even though those restrictions would pose absolutely no problem in the United States.

Examples of How Trade Secrets Are Treated Differently Throughout the World

Every country, whether a common law or civil code jurisdiction, treats trade secrets and the protection of corporate information differently. It is impractical to catalog here the multiple approaches from around the world. For those interested in specific countries or geographic regions, there are many excellent research materials available in public law libraries. Just to emphasize how varied legal structures are, a number of brief sketches follow.

The European Economic Community

Member countries of the European Economic Community (EEC), with the exception of the United Kingdom, are civil code jurisdictions. While each member of the EEC has its own laws, the EEC itself has a code governing the actions of EEC members. The statutes controlling the operation of the EEC reflect a strong bias against commercial agreements among companies which tend to restrict competition within the Common Market. Most of the guidelines that have been promulgated by the EEC Commission, the official regulating body of the EEC, concern patent or trademark law with few official pronouncements regarding licensing, transfer of know-how, and trade secrets. Although trade secret licensing agreements are subject to EEC laws when the agreements affect trade among the participating countries, there is no solid body of law which addresses the protection of trade secrets within the EEC. Businessmen should proceed cautiously. Nevertheless, certain guidelines for trade secrets owners can be gleaned from unofficial Commission proclamations and a limited number of Commission decisions.

The legal basis for trade secret protection under the EEC lies in the legal theory of unfair competition rather than in patent, copyright, or trademark law. A legal action to protect trade secrets in the EEC is based on either a claim under a contract or a claim that trade secrets were stolen or wrongfully used. The threshold determination before any protection can be granted is whether the information is in fact secret and whether the information is of practical commercial or industrial importance. Regarding secrecy, once the information becomes a matter of public knowledge, the agreement between licensor and licensee is no longer enforceable. Significantly, most agreements entered into with a company in an EEC country for use there must first be cleared by the EEC Commission. This is quite different from procedures within the United States. Thus, current EEC directives are very relevant.

If information is shown to be a trade secret, there are several general statements possible regarding protection and licensing of trade secrets among EEC countries. First, an attempt to consummate an exclusive agreement between a non-EEC company and a company in a EEC country may be objectionable to the EEC Commission if the agreement is viewed as a restriction of technology among the member countries of the EEC. However, when an exclusive agreement concerns only a small part of the market, it is likely the agreement will be upheld. Second, if an exclusive agreement is deemed as a necessary method to introduce a new, innovative technology into the EEC, the agreement will be upheld for a reasonable amount of time. Third, territorial restrictions in licenses which stop the licensee from distributing products made from the licensed information to other Common Market countries is generally objectionable because of a negative impact on the EEC as a whole. Finally, anti-competition clauses in trade agreements are disfavored by the EEC Commission because they impede technical progress and negatively affect commerce between Common Market countries. An agreement not containing any of the above restrictions and not opposed by the EEC Commission will enable a trade secret owner to bind a licensee to secrecy and to forbid disclosure of the trade secrets. Requiring a licensee to pay royalties on the products produced from know-how is also permissible in the EEC so long as the information remains secret and not part of the common public knowledge.

One unique aspect of trade secret protection among EEC companies vis-a-vis American companies concerns protection afforded chemical manufacturers. Both the United States and the EEC have promulgated laws regulating the use of hazardous chemical substances. Ironically, a recent EEC directive appears to afford owners of chemical trade secrets better protection than the American counterpart measure. Thus, chemical manufacturers may find themselves exporting their products to the EEC rather than to the United States due to the difference in trade secret protection available.

While the laws of the EEC apply when commerce among the participating countries is affected, the individual EEC countries have their own bodies of law. A brief review of the relevant laws in France, Germany, and Italy illustrates the different methods used to protect and govern licensing of trade secrets. France has long recognized the existence of the need for protection of trade secrets. While France differentiates between "secrets de fabrique" (i.e., secrets relating primarily to the manufacturing process or equipment) and "secrets de commerce" (i.e., secrets relating to internal communications regarding financial predictions, sales plans, bookkeeping, and contract disputes), both types of secrets can be protected. Although the French civil code does not specifically contain a provision for unfair competition actions, an action can be maintained in tort or contract. The French criminal code has for a long time contained a provision to punish employees and others who misappropriate trade secrets. Interestingly, French civil courts have the authority to issue injunctions if they desire.

Germany has similar statutory provisions plus some case law regarding protection of trade secrets. Germany has promulgated both the Unfair Competition Law and the Civil Code which provide both criminal and civil penalties for misappropriation or disclosure of trade secrets. Although the Italian civil and criminal codes both contain provisions regarding misappropriation of secret information, there is a paucity of case law or legislation in this area.

Therefore, American businessmen who seek to enter into licensing agreements involving trade secrets and know-how with a company in any EEC country must first check the relevant EEC law, because the EEC law will preempt individual country law when commerce among EEC countries is affected. Since there are few official guidelines, an American company should proceed cautiously before selling, licensing, or transferring trade secrets into any EEC country. Although some EEC countries, such as France and Germany, offer statutory protection by way of criminal or civil penalties within their borders, the agreement is first subject to EEC law and that law is still in the developmental stage.

Japan

Although Japan possesses a comprehensive civil law system, no Japanese civil code statute specifically deals with trade secrets or the ways by which trade secrets may be protected. Neither the Japanese Civil Code nor the Japanese Criminal Code has any defined mechanism capable for punishing those who have made unauthorized use of trade secrets. This is not to suggest that the Japanese are strangers to commercial and industrial trade secrets. They are bought, sold, licensed, and bartered every day. The unique aspect of Japanese law is that trade secrets are not considered as property in a legal sense. This means the Japanese Civil Code provisions which protect property from being stolen or misappropriated do not apply.

For a person who steals the trade secrets of another in Japan, there are some legal theories outside the code which make it theoretically possible to ask Japanese courts for relief. The Japanese Civil Code contains a provision for general tort actions and remedies. Under this provision an owner of trade secrets can seek damages for losses resulting from misuse of the trade secret. The Code also contains a provision for injunctive relief but, unfortunately from an American perspective, Japanese courts are reluctant to act in this area. The Japanese legal system has very few lawyers and litigation is considered only as a *last* resort.

The incidence of an employee stealing trade secrets from an employer is very rare in Japan, because the occurrence of Japanese employees leaving their employers to work for competitors is still a rarity. The phenomenon of moving from one job to another is totally opposed to the traditional Japanese lifetime employment concept. Nevertheless, there is a trend to allow an employer to bind an employee by contract from disclosing trade secrets during the term of employment and for a limited time thereafter. There are, however, few court decisions in this area, so it is not certain whether this type of protection will be continually afforded the employer who wishes to prevent his employees from disclosing trade secrets.

For the American company attempting to enter into an agreement with a Japanese firm to license trade secrets or know-how, there generally is no difficulty when the trade secrets are transferred in exchange for a cash payment. If, however, the know-how is granted for an exchange in kind, i.e., shares in the licensee's company or a grantback of a license, there may be difficulties due to the requirement of prior governmental approval. The Japanese government retains the right to approve or disapprove of these agreements based on whether or not they further the national interest.

Latin America

The treatment of employees, agents, and partners in Latin American countries can be particularly complex. Although most of these countries have criminal and civil code provisions prohibiting an employee from stealing or selling important trade secrets, criminal penalties are very light. Notably, these provisions are frequently limited to the protection or disclosures of industrial formulations and do not extend to the protection of commercial trade secrets such as consumer lists or suppliers. While customer informational lists would be considered trade secrets and protectable within the United States, most Latin American civil code jurisdictions do not agree. This makes planning and operations in these countries more difficult. You should also watch out for the local courts. The possibility of obtaining an injunction in a Latin American country against a national who is an employee is so remote as to be an unrealistic remedy in all but the most extreme situations.

While the principles just discussed are the general rule in most Latin American countries, there are exceptions. For instance, in Mexico both the criminal and civil code provisions offer some additional protection for owners of trade secrets. The Mexican criminal code prohibits a person from unlawfully or fraudulently obtaining a profit from another. The code also makes it unlawful for a person to disclose trade secrets obtained during the course of employment without consent of the employer. Both the criminal and civil code establish mechanisms to help owners of trade secrets either through some sort of restitution or a return to the status quo.

Colombia is unique in that its criminal code provides severe penalties in the form of fines or imprisonment for one who discloses a trade secret. Peru offers additional protection for owners of trade secrets in the form of a petition to a governmental agency specifically established to provide quick relief and with the authority to issue injunctive relief.

Most Latin American countries will enforce a contract between an employee and employer prohibiting the employee from disclosing trade secrets either during or after his course of employment. If this information later becomes public knowledge through no fault of the employee, the contract will no longer be enforceable. However, a covenant not to compete between an employer and employee after employment terminates, is not enforceable in most Latin American countries. The only Latin American country which might uphold such a covenant not to compete is Argentina, but the length of the covenant should be restricted to a limited time after employment terminates. The only certain advice is to seek the best possible legal advice in the country where trade secrets are and hope for the best.

International Contracts—Points to Consider

When entering into international contracts for establishing joint ventures, licensing agreements, or operations involving trade secrets in a foreign country, there are a number of basic considerations not to be overlooked. These are important regardless of whether the foreign country has a common law or a civil code system.

Which Law Will Apply?

In most situations, the law of the United States will be more favorable to an American trade secret owner than the law of a foreign jurisdiction. While not a good idea in all cases, during negotiations you should consider asking for an agreement that United States law will control the interpretation of the contracts. For example, in the Federal Republic of Germany treatment of distributors as defined by the German Code can be waived if the contract signed by the parties stipulates the law of another jurisdiction will apply. Remember, a contractual agreement providing that United States law will resolve disputes will, nevertheless, be unenforceable in many civil law countries because of local statutes protecting local citizens.

Definition of Trade Secrets

As noted earlier, many civil jurisdictions' commercial codes do contain definitions of trade secrets, commercial information, proprietary information, and industrial secrets. If possible, define in your contracts what specific types of information the contracting parties consider to be trade secrets and are protected by the contract. In the event there is a clearly written contract signed by both parties, foreign courts may give the benefit of the doubt to clear contract language freely adopted by both parties.

The Resolution of Disputes

As a general rule, our courts are impartial in their administration of justice in purely commercial litigation. A foreign person or corporation will have equal standing and opportunity to be heard with a United States citizen. This is not always the case in foreign countries where a national of that country is embroiled in litigation. Recognizing this, if a dispute arises in a foreign country, it is advisable to resolve it outside of that country. International commercial arbitration is a common provision in international contracts. For an American company, the best approach is not to insist on United States courts but rather to agree to resolve disputes in an impartial third country. While some civil law countries require that in all contract disputes their laws and tribunals will decide the issue, it never hurts to try to find an impartial forum.

The Ownership of After-Developed Technology

Because few civil law jurisdictions have reached the level of legal protection available for trade secrets under United States law, it is unlikely that a foreign law will address the issue of what happens to the ownership and control of new technology or trade secrets developed during a joint venture. Where a foreign commercial code is silent on the issue, well-drafted contractual provisions on how to handle newly developed technology should benefit the American partner if a problem later arises.

Antitrust Laws and Trade Secrets Outside the United States

At the turn of the century, the United States Congress passed major antitrust laws to prevent monopolization, price-fixing, and other forms of conduct considered to be harmful to our free market system. The legislative purpose was to insulate the American consumer against corporate activities he could not protect himself against. For many years United States exporters have worried that our antitrust laws might be enforced against them even though the activities they were engaged in were carried out solely in international markets. In response to strong pressure from a broad constituency, *The Export Trading Company Act of 1982* (ETCA) became law. Title IV of the

ETCA known as the "Foreign Trade Antitrust Improvements Act of 1982" amended two major federal antitrust laws by more clearly defining how they apply to activities outside the United States. The ETCA is of some help to American companies in planning their international activities dealing with trade secrets. Title III of the ETCA went even further by permitting United States exporters and those involved in joint ventures with trade secrets to seek prior governmental approval of their activities in foreign markets to avoid antitrust exposure. The point to be emphasized is that the licensing, the sale, or joint venturing with trade secrets overseas may have antitrust implications, so they must be examined before a final contract is entered into.

American companies must also be aware of foreign antitrust and anti-competition laws, particularly in the European Economic Community (EEC) and individual countries within the EEC. Individual EEC countries have passed restrictive statutes to prevent trade secrets from being used in ways which harm competition. The EEC anti-competitive statutes oppose trade secret limitations. Thus, combinations and exclusive arrangements involving commercially valuable trade secret technology among private parties should not ignore the existence of antitrust and anti-competition laws. Therefore, merely clearing the antitrust hurdles of United States laws is not enough in foreign markets.

Unique Aspects of Trade Secrets for High-Tech Companies

While all companies have trade secrets, high-tech companies are particularly vulnerable to a loss of trade secrets. This chapter analyzes the unique needs of high-tech ventures and the pitfalls to avoid.

The Nature of Trade Secrets for the High-Tech Companies and Why They Are Most Sensitive

All companies, regardless of size or business activity, possess commercially valuable trade secrets, but technology is generally a less critical element for companies in mature industries. Capital requirements and access to assured sources of supply frequently outweigh trade secrets in importance for mature industrial concerns. The story is far different for the high-tech company. Trade secrets play a linchpin role for high-tech companies. Since the cost of lack of diligence can be catastrophic, companies with high-tech secrets must become sensitized to their particular needs. There are seven factors that make trade secrets particularly critical for high-tech ventures.

Factor One: The Commercial Life of Trade Secrets for High-Tech Companies

In the ninteenth century, inventions were expected to have long commercial lives before new inventions or improvements replaced their utility. This long-life expectancy more than justified the equity investment needed to fully develop and market products. The high-tech company of the 1980s is faced with a different reality.

The highly competitive nature of most high-tech industries in the United States and around the world is a reflection of how many talented innovators there are and their broad geographic dispersal. Since new inventions and developments can have a commercial life of only one or two years, profits must be made quickly or they will be lost to competition. Secrecy and speed become the two requisite elements in the inexorable race for profitable commercial exploitation.

The ability to keep an innovation secret until it is actually ready for the market is particularly important for smaller high-tech companies that rely on a single product or a narrow range of products.

Factor Two: The Unavailability of Patent and Copyright Protection in Many High-Tech Ventures

The protection offered by patents and copyrights is useless to many high-tech industries. By their very nature, patents and copyrights are not capable of protecting many of the genuine innovations that have emerged in the last decade. For example, the law in the area of computer software is truly in an evolutionary state. Courts and scholars are now struggling with the legal issues of when computer programs are copyrightable and the scope of the actual protection copyrights can provide. Some lawyers today advise their clients to shield computer software under the trade secret laws and at the same time file for a copyright. Trade secret protection and copyright protection are not compatible. Trade secret protection assumes that secrecy is the best method to stop unauthorized disclosure. Copyright protection demands publication. Attempting to reconcile these approaches appears to be a mistake. Outside the computer software area, the bottom line is that there is no real choice for many high-tech industries between statutory (copyright and patent) protection and trade secrets. Trade secrets are the only viable alternative. The lack of choice reinforces the importance high-tech companies should place on trade secrets as the only reliable avenue for protecting key corporate information.

Factor Three: The Risk of the Key High-Tech Employee

Most high-tech companies will rise or fall on new innovations and improvements developed by their technical staffs. Unlike the more traditional industries in the United States, where the hourly laborer plays an important part in the viability of the company, the future for a high-tech company often rests in the hands of a few key individuals. This inordinate concentration of power is a serious problem for the high-tech company. The loss of an indispensable employee through his voluntary resignation to join a competitor is an unpleasant reality for a high-tech company's chief operating officer. Unfortunately, trade secrets frequently depart along with the employee.

The small high-tech company is particularly at the mercy of the key innovative employee. The theft of many, if not all, of a small company's trade secrets may be accomplished by a single employee in a short period of time. This vulnerability to theft can be minimized by a comprehensive corporate trade secret program but never totally eliminated. It simply reinforces the need for a multilevel corporate-wide plan to protect trade secrets. Small companies which ignore unpleasant prospects end up paying a very dear price for their inattention.

*Factor Four: The Role of Marketing and Financial
Information for the High-Tech Venture*

Successful high-tech companies in a truly competitive market place cannot rely on a new product's selling itself simply because it is cheaper or technically superior to existing products on the market. Numerous high-tech ventures fail because they lack the marketing skills and financial support required to sustain an effective marketing effort. When the factor of rapid obsolescence is added to the formula, the ability to sell and price a product correctly is crucial to survival.

High-tech companies must learn to understand that corporate information on future marketing plans can be as important as technological advances. The marketing strategy of IBM Corporation in late 1983 with the introduction of its IBM PC jr. personal computer is a case in point. Weeks before the actual announcement, competitors were unsure whether IBM actually had the IBM PC jr. computer, what its capabilities were, and when it would be introduced into the market. IBM was able to orchestrate its retention and release of information to create a dramatic public commencement for the marketing campaign to sell its new computer line. The rumors were enough to depress the stock of a number of IBM's competitors in the personal computer field for some time.

Financial statistics and projections by themselves can tell competitors everything they need to know about future strategies. Technical people are more likely to be disciplined on the need to protect their technological trade secrets than are financially oriented employees. Those with access to financial information often fail to appreciate the critical nature of the information they create and are to control.

*Factor Five: The Problems of Outside Suppliers
and Subcontractors*

High-tech companies commonly turn to outside suppliers and subcontractors to help meet the time demands for bringing a new product to market. Subcontracting may be preferable to internal expansion where long-term prospects for a product are uncertain. This is frequently the case in the computer field where subcontractors actually manufacture the subassemblies. While some companies who are sensitive to their trade secrets at first set up parameters and procedures for trade secrets revealed to outside contractors and suppliers, their initial efforts at protection tend to be ignored as new suppliers and contractors are used. Again, it is negligence that poses a primary threat to trade secrets. The weak link often is the failure to designate a single employee who is charged with overall responsibility to assure continuing compliance with an existing trade secret policy. The quickly growing, successful company is the prime violator.

Factor Six: The Reality of Trade Secret Espionage for High-Tech Companies

Success in established manufacturing sectors is largely dependent on capital-intensive equipment, assured sources of reliable supply, and extensive marketing organizations. Corporate espionage is not an everyday occurrence. Competitors undertake planned corporate espionage only if there is a dire need. The opposite is true in high-tech industries. The right technology at the right time for high-tech companies can mean the difference between profitability and bankruptcy. Corporate graveyards are littered with the bones of companies that lost their competitive technological edge over the last few years. Espionage should not be a surprise; it should be anticipated and not allowed to happen.

Factor Seven: High-Tech Companies Producing Technologies with Military Applications

Where companies have technologies with direct or indirect military applications, the threat of outside interference emanates from both competitors and foreign governments seeking those technologies. Foreign governments use a variety of mechanisms, including front organizations both domestic and foreign, that try to buy, license, or obtain trade secrets. While the United States government has recently beefed up its programs designed to stop national security-related espionage, it is impossible to guess how much goes undetected. The high-tech company with trade secrets of value to foreign governments must be super sensitive to the risks. The failure of internal security can result in the permanent loss of government contracts which is a very high price to pay.

The Profile of High-Tech Employees: Are They Unique?

Many who are responsible for running high-tech companies fail to appreciate the unique nature of their employees. The fast pace of growing high-tech companies results in the hiring of those employees who will be *least* inclined to protect corporate trade secrets. High-tech companies should devote major attention to those employees who are responsible for innovating, designing, and administering the development, production, and marketing of new products and services. What follows is a profile of these employees. It will help high-tech companies understand the possible problem areas. If a company finds that its employees share the characteristics described below, it should be particularly concerned that an existing trade secret program is adequate to deal with the risks.

The Youth and Mobility of High-Tech Innovators

There are few middle-aged high-tech innovators unless they started the company. Notably in the computer field, the most valuable technical innovators may be under the age of 30 or almost certainly under the age of 40. The youth of these employees means they may possess a different set of drives, expectations and, in the opinion of some, ethics. The youthful innovator without traditional strong family ties, a specific geographic orientation, or financial responsibilities has no permanent base. This means the employee is highly mobile and without binding attachments to a particular company or geographic area. Financial incentives are an important weapon in the hands of competitors who use dollars to attract high-tech innovators away. This situation differs radically from the Japanese experience where long-term loyalty to a particular company is the norm and job performance considered a matter of ethical responsibility. The employer in the high-tech company should never assume his youthful innovators are happy or will be content to remain with the company over a long period of time when their skills are in high demand and readily marketable anywhere.

The Bias Toward Innovation and Against Administration

Innovators in high-tech companies are paid to create. Management and administrative skills are not expected and are rarely present. Administration as a skill is not viewed as important and is intellectually demeaned. While trade secret rules and procedures are necessary, innovators do not appreciate the reasons for trade secret protection. Trade secret programs appear bureaucratic and unnecessary. An employer has to conscientiously explain to the innovators the important reasons why the procedures exist and why they must not be ignored. In short, innovative employees tend to be non-systems-oriented. Continuing education and reinforcement are essential if realistic compliance is expected.

The Short-Term Orientation Syndrome

Because of the emphasis on innovation and growth within the high-tech companies, most top employees with those ventures are paid based upon short-term goals and objectives. Since trade secret protection is a long-term activity which does not yield identifiable profits and achievements, a danger exists. Trade secret protection as a purely conservative, defensive procedure frequently fails to receive a high priority in both attention and resources from the top executives.

The General Ignorance of the Legal Mechanisms to Protect Trade Secrets

While most employees involved with innovation and technical projects will not recognize the overall importance of trade secrets to their employer's survival, they will understand their overall value. Invariably, while they recognize their own personal contributions to corporate innovation, they tend to regard legal mechanisms to protect trade secrets as a nuisance. As a result, the "legalisms" of secrecy agreements, restrictive covenants, and methods of trade secret protection are ignored, if not directly opposed within the organization. This attitude results in very serious consequences.

Observations on the Rapidly Growing High-Tech Company

Ironically, the rapidly growing high-tech company may be its own worst enemy. If trade secrets have played an important role in development of the corporation, its continued expansion will increasingly depend upon a secure legal umbrella over its existing trade secrets. Understanding why such a venture is particularly susceptible to trade secret loss is a prerequisite to minimizing those risks.

The Phenomenon of Rapid Growth and Hiring Policies

It is a common evolutionary pattern for a high-tech company to be formed out of the ideas generated by a few innovating individuals.

The core individuals discover a valuable idea, set up a small company, the company takes off, and the company is faced with a problem—success. The company is forced to expand its size in order to satisfy rapidly growing demands for its products or services. To maintain a high-tech leadership edge, the company must be able to attract top technicians and professionals. Under these circumstances, hiring in response to immediate needs is carried out on an emergency, haphazard basis. Attention to detail is overlooked in the rush to fill vacancies. The company refuses to take the time to carefully examine job candidates. Not infrequently, high-tech companies find the integrity of their trade secrets compromised by those employees hired during periods of rapid growth. These employees will not share the sense of corporate loyalty and achievement the company founders expect. This makes the highly mobile professional who joins the growing high-tech company a very real potential risk to corporate trade secrets.

The Reality of Outmoded Systems for Trade Secret Control

When a small company begins operations, it is common for a simple, workable system to control trade secrets to be set in place. While the company remains small, maintains a limited number of employees, and operates a single physical plant, a rudimentary trade secret system will in all likelihood work. When the company enters into a rapid growth phase, circumstances force it to handle a multitude of priorities simultaneously. When some type of trade secret system is already in place, updating the system will ordinarily be far down the list of corporate priorities. An outmoded corporate trade secret program is a ticking time bomb. Every growing high-tech company must place protection of its trade secrets at or near the top of its list of its corporate priorities. An outmoded system is little better than none at all.

Dealing with Related Outside Parties and Trade Secrets

Every company experiencing rapid growth finds it periodically needs skills it does not possess such as: outside financial advisors, equity investors, consultants of all kinds, bankers, and accountants. A company may also need new subcontractors and outside suppliers for unforeseen production demands. The continuing exposure to outsiders invariably means trade secrets become available to them as those outsiders perform their designated roles. While control of trade secrets within one's own corporate structure is difficult, control is increasingly more complicated as outsiders and their employees gain access to trade secrets. Where outside parties and consultations dealing with trade secrets are unavoidable, a uniform, concrete and continuously updated approach is absolutely necessary.

The Typical High-Tech Corporate Priorities— Innovation and Sale

The growing company experiences rapidly increasing sales for its products and services. Often, it is unprepared for the demands accompanying growth. While future sales of products cannot be accurately predicted in any industry, it is exceptionally difficult to forecast them in very competitive high-tech areas. Products are quickly outmoded by a new technology, so a premium is placed on the need for continuing innovation efforts to develop new products and to improve existing products. High sales volume is needed to underwrite the expenses of innovation. The result is great emphasis on the development and sale of new products while all else appears unimportant. In this atmosphere, trade secret protective measures are bound to receive less attention and problems will result. While trade secret protection will rarely exceed innovation on the list of priorities, it should be closely linked.

Do All High-Tech Companies Get the Right Legal Advice?

Companies can outgrow their lawyers in the same way companies outgrow physical facilities during an expansion period. A law firm which initially assisted a high-tech venture to become incorporated may lack the sophistication to handle the myriad complicated legal issues facing rapidly growing high-tech ventures. Every high-tech company should periodically ask itself whether its existing legal counsel is the right firm to render advice on trade secrets and the other unique kinds of problems common to high-tech companies.

The Impact of Joint Ventures and Licensing Opportunities for Growing High-Tech Companies

The greatest risk any high-tech company runs is to lose trade secrets and its competitive edge at the same time. Nevertheless, many growing high-tech companies require help if they are to reach their potential. Help may require more than adding additional employees, buying more equipment, changing subcontractors, borrowing more money, or hiring consultants. Forming a joint venture between a small high-tech venture and a more established company is one method of rapidly acquiring needed resources by the smaller company. Joint ventures, however, are a two-edged sword. Joint venture partners may supply those services or elements which a rapidly growing company does not possess. For example, a high-tech company designs and manufactures a switching device with numerous possible applications in the telecommunications industry but may fail to penetrate a particular market because it lacks a broad-based distributor/sales network with existing contacts with major potential users for the new device. Forming a joint venture with a second company with a proven distribution and sales structure can make the difference between success and failure for the high-tech company. A major roadblock for the growing high-tech company is that it often lacks the background, expertise, and personnel to properly seek out the best joint venture partner.

The same analysis applies to trade secret licensing opportunities for the high-tech company. It is not unusual for a high-tech company to be approached by a company asking for a license to the smaller company's technology so that the company can use the technology to manufacture and sell in a defined geographic market. Too often, inexperienced high-tech companies execute license agreements without a clear appreciation of the many risks that go along with the bargain. Chapter Six was entirely devoted to solving these problems.

Conclusion

In conclusion, all high-tech companies face particularly serious consequences from the mishandling of trade secrets. The high-tech venture, particularly the new and growing operation, must educate itself to the pitfalls which do exist before acting if it hopes to survive in the long run.

10

The Legal Strategy and Your Weapons to Stop Trade Secret Misuse and Theft

If the worst happens, you must be prepared to react immediately to minimize damage to trade secrets. Chapter Ten is a game plan for the top executive to use in combating trade secret theft or misappropriation.

The Philosophy of Punishing Trade Secret Violators

A trade secret has value only if it remains secret. Once a trade secret becomes known to the public either through independent discovery, reverse engineering, publication, employee errors, or industrial espionage, a non-culpable competitor may use it without fear of being held legally responsible. Up to this point, this book has examined different strategies to preserve valuable trade secrets from disclosure. This chapter will present specific techniques to avoid a trade secret defense system breakdown and to repair damage when it occurs. In order to do this, corporate managers must act decisively to stop improper disclosures of trade secrets and be ready to utilize a broad arsenal of legal weapons.

It is highly desirable for your company to develop a reputation as a company that vigorously protects its trade secrets. This is an essential element in planning a trade secret strategy. Your employees and your competitors must believe you are prepared to take action immediately against any trade secret violator and to "pull all stops" in pursuing suspected disclosure problems. A strategy of this kind does much to deter present and potential trade secret misappropriators. Trade secret litigation is not always the sole option. The goal of trade secret litigation is to prevent or to halt trade secret losses. There are alternative steps that fall short of the lengthy, expensive litigation process. Your company must in advance implement a review procedure so that when a problem arises the decision of whether to commence litigation is almost automatic.

As a first step, develop and coordinate your company policy with your attorneys *before* a problem arises. Have a legal contingency plan in place that can be immediately implemented if a trade secret problem surfaces. In your contingency planning efforts, evaluate the extent of financial resources your company is willing to commit if valuable trade secrets are threatened. Locate in advance experienced, tough litigation attorneys who are familiar with handling trade secret theft cases. Not all trial attorneys have the unique skills needed for difficult trade secret cases. Review your contingency plan with outside counsel and ask for their advice on the legal remedies available. Your range of responses can vary from jurisdiction to jurisdiction. Remember, timing is absolutely critical to trade secret protection. Arrangements must be made before there is a disclosure problem.

Attacking Trade Secret Theft with Litigation

Early Detection

The first step in preparation for litigation is the early detection of trade secret theft. Maintain close contact with your most critically valuable employees and those outsiders you allow authorized access to your secret information. On a continuing basis, keep key employees and related parties informed of company policy and initiate periodic checks to assess if corporate policies are being followed.

Preliminary Considerations

After a wrongful trade secret disclosure is discovered, the second step in preparation for litigation is to balance a variety of factors. Weigh the advantages against the disadvantages of bringing suit. First, evaluate the trade secret in light of the following economic considerations: (1) the original developmental costs; (2) its present and prospective market worth if secrecy is preserved; (3) its market value if the trade secret is fully disclosed; (4) the extent to which the secret is known by others in the business and by your employees; and (5) the extent and cost of present and projected security measures to protect the secret from further disclosure.

Second, assess how litigation will affect your company in the following areas.

(1) Employee morale will suffer if the misappropriator is not punished.

(2) Your business reputation may be affected by adverse public reaction if a suit is instituted and later dropped or lost. Conversely, business reputation may be hurt if the violator is not pursued.

(3) Litigation can potentially risk public disclosure of trade secrets. However, trade secrets may be preserved by asking the court to establish various protective measures to limit disclosure of your secret information to the immediate litigation only.

(4) The ordinary course of any business is invariably disrupted by litigation. Employees involved in active preparation for litigation, gathering information, and testifying about the trade secret lose otherwise productive time.

Finally, evaluate the likelihood of successful litigation. Consider the following: (1) the relative strengths and weaknesses of your claim of trade secret misappropriation; (2) the possibility of speedy relief without disclosure; and (3) the amount of attorney's fees and who will ultimately pay them

The Elements Necessary for Successful Litigation

Prior to commencing suit, review the common elements of a trade secret action and evaluate the strength of your claim. Generally, a trade secret owner must prove three things: (1) the existence and ownership of a trade secret; (2) facts showing that the misappropriator of trade secrets learned of the trade secret by improper means and wrongfully disclosed or used the trade secret in an unauthorized manner; and (3) the owner of trade secrets was damaged by the disclosure.

Many courts have decided trade secrets can include, among other things, computer software, chemical formulae, industrial processes, pricing information, sources for supplies, customer lists, and marketing information. One incontestable precondition to trade secret protection is that the owner has taken reasonable precautions to maintain its secrecy. A trade secret owner must be prepared to describe to a court the specific security measures taken, including contractual relationships. The degree of secrecy must be such that it is very difficult for others to obtain the information without using improper means.

For example, in one case, a high-tech company imposed a corporate policy that specially designed computer programs in the field of direct mail advertising must remain in-house and were not to be shown to outsiders. The court decided this was sufficient precaution and justified reliance that the employees and officers would not reveal the confidential information. However, in another trade secret case protection was not granted to an athletic mouthguard company's customer list, where the company could not prove its customer lists were kept secret rather than developed from the general store of the employee's contacts and knowledge built up over several years of sales.

A trade secret owner must next establish for the court that the misappropriator actually used or intended to use secret information in a wrongful manner. For example, the most common wrongdoer is the ex-employee who discloses or uses trade secrets to establish a new business or to join your competitor's business. Your employee is induced by a competitor to reveal secrets and breach his confidential relationship. Other potential culprits are joint venture partners, independent contractors, agents, or purchasers who wrongfully use or disclose secret information that was disclosed in confidence. The most readily understood example is wrongful appropriation through industrial espionage. This method, unfortunately, is difficult to detect and prove.

The last element to prove is the damage resulting from trade secret theft or misuse. Two basic measures of damages are possible; the owner's lost sales and damage to reputation or the misappropriator's profits from using the trade secrets. When the measure of damages is the misappropriator's profits, a business consideration is the financial condition of the misappropriator and the possibility at the time of trial that the thief is unable to pay any judgment.

Only after weighing these factors can trade secret owners make a realistic economic decision by comparing the value of the trade secret against the potential adverse impact of litigation. Once your decision to litigate is made, do not overlook an important opportunity. Give your employees maximum information about your legal action against the misappropriator. This is an opportunity to reinforce employee awareness of your company policy on trade secrets and to emphasize that no cost will be spared to punish the slightest violation of company policy.

Legal Weapons to Protect Trade Secrets— Three Basic Approaches

If it makes sense to litigate, what are the legal remedies a trade secret owner has available to use against wrongful misappropriators? In most jurisidctions the owner of a trade secret has an arsenal of potential legal weapons. Three approaches are available: (1) injunctive relief; (2) a civil lawsuit for damages; and (3) criminal proceedings. Each remedy will be briefly explained below and then examined in greater detail later in the chapter.

Injunctions

The most commonly used legal weapon in trade secret litigation is injunctive relief. Generally, an injunction is an order by a court that directs someone to act or to refrain from acting in a specified way. An injunction granted in trade secret cases will generally prohibit a person or company from using trade secrets as well as disclosing them to others. Injunctions are designed to prevent disclosure for a specified period of time. This is usually measured by the time reasonably necessary to protect the trade secret owner's interest. There are three generic types of injunctions: the temporary restraining order (the TRO); the preliminary injunction; and the permanent injunction.

The Temporary Restraining Order

A temporary restraining order is an injunction granted without prior notice to the defendant. The trade secret owner must show that his need for relief is so compelling that there is no time to notify his opponent of the court hearing. It is common to use this procedure to prevent an employee from leaving that day and taking trade secrets with him to another employer. If the court is satisfied immediate action must be taken to protect a trade secret owner, it will grant an order that will effectively stop the misappropriator's actions for a limited time of up to ten days. Within this short time, a second hearing is held. At this hearing the defendant is present. The value of the injunction to the trade secret owner is weighed against the burden to the defendant caused by the injunction.

The Preliminary Injunction

A preliminary injunction is similar to a temporary restraining order because each is granted as an emergency measure before a full hearing can be held. However, in a preliminary injunction, the defendant receives notice that a hearing will be held and a judge will be asked to rule on the motion for preliminary injunction. The trade secret owner can establish his case informally by presenting sworn statements, but in a preliminary injunction hearing the misappropriator is also given an opportunity to present evidence. If the misappropriator is able to rebut the sworn statements, the trade secret owner must then furnish additional proof to justify his request for relief. A preliminary injunction can continue in duration until the dispute is finally resolved by the court with the issuance of a permanent injunction or by dissolution of the preliminary injunction.

The Permanent Injunction

A permanent injunction is the third basic form of injunction. It is granted after a full hearing and opportunity by both sides to present all relevant evidence. The permanent injunction is intended to be the final solution to the dispute rather than a temporary or emergency one.

Damages

Aside from the injunction route, trade secret owners may recover money from a wrongful misappropriator. This legal weapon, a civil lawsuit for damages, is available either with injunctive relief or separately. One reason to seek damages separately is to salvage rather than protect the trade secret's value if the secret has already been disclosed to the public. An action to recover money damages, in some cases, may be the only relief that will adequately compensate the owner for this loss.

Monetary damages in a civil action reflect the nature of the wrongful misappropriation of trade secrets. For example, employee secrecy agreements, described in earlier chapters, may contain liquidated damage clauses providing for a particular amount of money to be paid by an employee who breaches the agreement. In some states liquidated damages can be enforced without showing the misappropriator acted in a particularly egregious manner. Agreements may also contain provisions requiring the payment of attorney's fees and interest when one has acted improperly. If the misappropriator's conduct is extremely outrageous and offensive, punitive damages are sometime available. Another legal remedy is for the court to force a misappropriator to pay over to the trade secret owner all the illegal profits made from the trade secrets.

Criminal Proceedings

A third legal weapon available to a trade secret owner is the opportunity to bring criminal sanctions against the misappropriator. Federal and state criminal statutes prohibit the misappropriation of trade secrets. Some state statutes have more teeth than others, so it is important to examine the proper state law which has jurisdiction. A criminal statute with teeth will apply to the theft of tangible plans and documents as well as to the theft of intangible information, such as that taken by memorization. Criminal sanctions and the other legal weapons will be examined in greater detail later.

Implementing a Trade Secret Recovery Procedure

Demand Return of the Secret Information Prior to Instituting Suit

To prevent disclosure of trade secrets by an ex-employee, it is necessary to seek immediate injunctive relief when you discover a failure in your precautionary procedures. Demand return of misappropriated information from the ex-employee when preliminary relief is sought to prevent a suspected disclosure. If you have not formally demanded that unauthorized and illegal practices cease and the information be returned, a court may refuse to grant relief. One technique to make such a demand is to prepare a copy of the complaint and send it to the ex-employee or his attorney before it is filed. This may prompt the ex-employee to settle and to return any secret information. There will be substantial savings by avoiding the litigation process.

Preserving Secrecy During Litigation

One major concern in trade secret litigation is that the secret will be disclosed at some time during trial. In order to prevent this, ask the court at the time your suit is filed to order that all papers in the case be preserved in secrecy; that outside spectators be barred from the court during trial; and all proceedings be held in a closed courtroom. Pleadings, depositions, transcripts, and any other material designated confidential, where possible under court procedures, should also be submitted to the court in sealed packages. Depending on the nature of the secret information, reference to the trade secret may be made without discussion of its internal structure. These measures help to preserve secrecy while the issue is resolved.

At the time of filing suit, it may be appropriate to ask the court to issue a writ of attachment permitting the trade secret owner to gain custody of any documents or tangible objects taken by the wrongful misappropriator. With this legal writ in hand, accompany the United States Marshall or Sheriff when the court papers (process) are served on the misappropriator. The person with a writ may search for and seize any of the misappropriated property that it lists. Everything recovered will be protected and useful at the trial.

Using the Injunction—The Blitzkreig Technique

Preliminary Relief: A Hypothetical Example

A preliminary injunction is the preferred approach because it can stop unauthorized disclosure *before* it occurs or it can immediately affect the potential violator. One reason for a trade secret owner to consider seeking a preliminary injunction is to prevent further disclosure if the misappropriator is undercapitalized or otherwise financially weak and attempts to pledge, transfer, or otherwise sell a process or design that includes your misappropriated secret information. If the secret information is disclosed to an innocent purchaser or user who paid value for the secret, in most cases the innocent purchaser or user will have no liability to you, so swift action is crucial!

Assume the following fact situations: (1) an employee with access to valuable trade secret information notifies you that he is leaving your company to work for a competitor; or (2) you discover a current employee is removing secret information and selling it to a competitor. What should you do? Immediate action is necessary. Prompt injunctive relief is the way to protect your trade secret property. A preliminary ex-parte injunction or temporary restraining order, as it is known in federal court, provides immediate "Blitzkreig" relief. It is possible to request a temporary injunction from a judge, obtain relief, and serve the ex-employee on his way out the door. The purpose of the temporary restraining order is to maintain the status quo until all the facts are later presented to the judge when a determination will be made as to the appropriateness of further legal relief. An injunction will prevent the misappropriator from utilizing the services of an employee or from pledging, transferring, or otherwise encumbering the trade secret without first giving notice to the trade secret owner.

The Preliminary Injunction and the Temporary Restraining Order

The immediate relief granted to a trade secret owner by a temporary restraining order will normally dissolve within ten days. This occurs in order to protect the defendant-misappropriator because immediate relief was granted without prior notification. The judge who granted the motion was presented with only one version of the facts. Of course, after the hearing the defendant is notified and given an opportunity to present his version of the facts to the judge at later injunctive hearings.

Generally, the preliminary injunction is a request to maintain the status quo during the time when all the facts are gathered, and will last until a final determination can be made. It is usually the most important part of the case because failure to obtain a preliminary injunction is a good indication that there will be a failure at the final hearing. When the final determination is made, the judge will either order some form of permanent relief or dissolve the preliminary injunction.

Legal Theories upon Which Courts May Respond

Before approaching any court for legal relief in a trade secret action, develop a basis or theory that supports your right to legal relief. The most frequently presented basis supporting trade secret litigation is that of a written (express) contract. Express contracts, as described in earlier chapters, are those agreements and covenants a trade secret owner should have his employees and related businesses employees sign. A well-drafted contract reduces the risk of an employee's taking advantage of his access to secret information and reduces the possibility of failing to get an injunction in court. To succeed, the agreement must generally be reasonable in length, time, and geographical area and not impose an undue hardship on the employee or outside related parties such as your subcontractors.

An action based upon an express contract is preferred because the parties had the opportunity to agree upon express restrictions on their own before there was a problem. However, the law can imply from facts surrounding the nature of the business and the relationship of the parties a prohibition against the betrayal of trust and confidence. The strongest protection here is found where a previously developed trade secret is disclosed to an employee so that the employee can perform his assigned duties. Where such a confidential relationship between the parties can be established, a court may imply there was a contract by the employee not to divulge trade secrets to third persons or to personally use those gained or discovered in the course of his employment. The weaker protection exists where the misappropriator originally developed the trade secret while using the resources of his employer.

A second legal basis supporting trade secrets litigation is a theory based upon tortious conduct that injury was caused by a breach of confidence. A "tort" is a legal term referring to a wrongful action by a person. A trade secret owner must show to a court that it had knowledge or information not generally known and that the information was communicated to an employee who wrongfully used the information in violation of the confidential disclosure. This theory focuses on the personal and confidential relationship of the parties at the time of disclosure.

A third legal basis upon which to institute a trade secret action is where a trade secret is viewed as a form of property, and cannot be taken or used without the owner's consent. This property-right theory comes in two forms, an intellectual property right intangible in form or a physical property right in the form of documents and plans. Physical trade secret information theft is the general basis for federal and state criminal actions.

Four Legal Elements Necessary to Get a Preliminary Injunction

A legal complaint asking for injunctive relief is prepared, filed, and presented to the judge who reviews the pleadings and listens to the attorneys. If the following four elements are proved, the judge has the power to grant injunctive relief.

1. *The trade secret owner will suffer irreparable harm if the injunction is not granted.* Irreparable harm is established by proving that monetary damages alone will not compensate the trade secret owner for the loss suffered or that it is impossible to ascertain the amount of damages accurately. This element is the key in trade secret cases since the nature of vital trade secrets is such that once disclosed a trade secret's value disappears and cannot be adequately measured in lost dollars.

2. *Granting the injunction will not have an injurious effect upon the general public.* The court balances the public's interest in unrestrained competition, against the possible injury to the trade secret owner.

3. *The inconvenience to the opposing party will be small compared to the immediate and certain loss to the trade secret owner if the injunction is denied.*

4. *The trade secret owner has a reasonable likelihood to succeed on the merits when each side presents all the facts at a full hearing.* To obtain injunctive relief, the trade secret owner must be prepared to demonstrate to the court that the trade secret misappropriator has shown, was about to, or was likely to disclose to a third party the secret information. Additionally, a trade secret owner must show that all reasonable efforts were taken to preserve the information's secrecy before the problem arose.

Many defendants argue that once the transfer of secret information was completed, the eggs were broken and the omelet cannot be unscrambled, so injunctive relief is not appropriate. However, the court can use the injunctive remedy as a broad power to preserve the status quo. The following sample injunctive order granted in a trade secret theft of computer software case illustrates this point:

The defendant cannot sell, transfer or disclose the whole or any part of the technology which defendant is unwilling or unable to extricate any changes made by defendant to any software supplied to it by plaintiff. The defendant, its directors, officers, employees agents, and all other persons acting in concert with them are restrained and enjoined from selling, transferring, or further disclosing to any third party any of the systems software developments and technology supplied by plaintiff to the defendant.

The Permanent Injunction—How a Preliminary Injunction Becomes Permanent

A permanent injunction is possible only after a full trial. The trial balances all the equities, examines the parties' conduct, and sorts out the nature of the interests involved. The judge has broad discretion in fashioning an appropriate remedy. Of course, the best remedy for the trade secret owner would be for the misappropriator to be forever barred from using the secret information and to impose this restraint before any disclosure was made to the competition. Often, however, injunctive relief prohibits a misappropriator or competitor who received the secret information from disclosing or developing the secret information for a limited period of time. This time period is usually measured by the amount of time necessary for a third party to "reverse engineer" or develop the trade secret information without any illegal assistance.

Damages and Other Remedies

What Damages Are and How to Prove Them

While injunctive relief is the most frequently sought remedy, monetary damages are available where there is a wrongful use of the owner's trade secrets. In order to recover damages for the misappropriation of trade secrets, the trade secret owner must prove the secrets were commercially used or sold in some way by the misappropriator. While the owner does not have to show that a misappropriator generated any profit, it must show the secret was used in some manner. This can be difficult because misappropriators usually keep their activities secret.

The measure of compensatory damages is determined at the time of filing suit. A trade secret plaintiff may demand recovery for damages actually incurred by the trade secret owner, including direct, profits, fixed overhead costs, and profits on spare parts and reorders. Proof of actual losses is frequently difficult and speculative in trade secret cases. Alternatively, the trade secret owner may demand recovery of the profits earned by the misappropriator. This achieves a twofold goal by requiring the misappropriator, who was the ultimate beneficiary of wrongful acts, to account for and disgorge its wrongfully earned profits, and at the same time serves to compensate the owner for the injury suffered. It is important to stress, though, in all cases, that the damages must be ascertainable and not purely speculative.

Seeking "Reasonable Royalties" for Stolen Trade Secrets

A reasonable royalty is an alternative measure of trade secret damages. This form of damages is appropriate and easily ascertainable if the trade secret owner has previously received royalties for use of the trade secret by persons other than the misappropriator. The reasonable royalty measure of damages is based upon the same royalty that was paid by the third party under his agreement with the trade secret owner.

Forcing the Misappropriator to "Disgorge" Profits

Damages may be measured by the amount of profits earned by the misappropriator from use of the trade secret. This amount is determined by performing an equitable accounting. If the misappropriator would not have made any profits without wrongfully using the secret information, the owner may recover *all* the illegal profits.

Recovery can be based upon the commercial advantage gained by the misappropriator. Under this legal theory, the court compares the cost to the misappropriator of using the trade secret to the cost that would have been borne if the same information had been developed by lawful means. For example, if a misappropriator gains or would have gained two-years' worth of profit by stealing a trade secret, a court could force the company to compensate the trade secret owner in the amount of two-years' profit.

Who Pays Attorney's Fees?

Generally, parties to litigation pay their own attorney's fees unless there is an express provision by contract or statutory law. In the absence of a statute, attorney's fees are recoverable only under special circumstances.

Special circumstances exist where a court concludes the appropriation of trade secrets was unconscionable, malicious, willful, and in bad faith. If the defendant's conduct evidences a blatant, bad faith violation of duty, fidelity, and loyalty to a trade secret owner, courts can decide that justice is served only if attorney's fees are awarded in addition to other damages. The trade secret plaintiff should always ask for payment of attorney's fees, but if the plaintiff's claim for misappropriation is itself determined to be in bad faith, the defendant may be entitled to recover attorney's fees.

Practically speaking, trade secret actions are generally settled prior to a full trial. As part of any settlement agreement, attorneys' fees are normally considered and included. Attorneys' fees are often substantial in trade secret litigation and should be viewed as an element of damages for settlement purposes. Recently, it was reported, Hitachi Ltd. agreed to pay IBM's legal fees (estimated in the seven-figure range) in connection with a law suit that charged Hitachi Ltd. had conspired to transport stolen IBM trade secret material to Japan.

What Are Punitive Damages?

Punitive damages are the cream on top of an award of compensatory damages. Punitive damages are rarely given by a court. They are awarded in excess of the actual damages incurred by the injured party and can greatly exceed the amount of compensatory damages. Trade secret owners may recover punitive damages only if it is proven the misappropriator's misconduct was willful and deliberate. Outrageous conduct is a commonly used term to describe conduct deserving of punitive damages.

Punitive damages are not recoverable for a trade secret legal action based strictly on breach of contract, unless the conduct constituting the breach is partially due to a breach of confidential relationship or tortious misappropriation. Courts have awarded punitive damages in cases where the misappropriator's activities were characterized as calculated, deliberate, reprehensible, and where the misappropriator clearly knew that substantial harm would be caused to the trade secret owner. When preparing to institute legal proceedings, review with counsel all forms of damages and include a claim for punitive damages if appropriate.

The Option of Criminal Sanctions

The least used but potentially most crippling legal weapon available to the trade secret owner—criminal sanction—is implemented in addition to the injunctive and civil damages remedies. Criminal sanctions under state and federal law are a relatively recent development. They can afford a viable means to punish and deter trade secret theft. This legal weapon attacks with equal devastation, the large corporate misappropriator and the smaller company. Because large corporations can afford to spend a large sum of money on trade secret civil litigation and smaller companies cannot, the criminal sanction actually may be a more effective means to punish the large corporate violator.

To properly analyze criminal trade secret law, each specific state statute must be reviewed because state laws vary in their characterization of trade secret theft as a crime. You should examine applicable state statutes during the development stage of your company's contingency plan. Don't forget to incorporate a reference to the relevant criminal statutes in any educational efforts to inform employees about the company policy regarding nondisclosure of trade secrets.

To implement state and federal proceedings against a wrongful misappropriation, the trade secret owner must file a complaint in state court with the local state prosecutor or in federal court with the United States Attorney's office. After this initial step, the trade secret owner, unlike his role in civil litigation, must relinquish control of the litigation process to the prosecutor. Be prepared that a state prosecutor or federal attorney will want access to corporate files that contain trade secret information in order to build a criminal case against the misappropriator.

Federal and State Law Claims

Criminal sanctions under federal law are available under two statutes: (1) the federal Transportation of Stolen Goods Statute, 18 U.S.C. §2314 and (2) the federal Mail Fraud Statute 18 U.S.C. §1341. Examine each of these federal statutes when implementing any trade secret theft contingency plan.

The federal Transportation of Stolen Goods Statute prohibits the transportation across state lines of "any goods, wares, merchandise, securities or money, of the value of $5,000.00 or more," by a person knowing that the merchandise is stolen. It is well settled that trade secrets qualify as "goods" under this statute. Two examples where criminal sanctions were imposed are: (1) the interstate transportation of misappropriated microorganisms and related documents used in the production of antibiotics and (2) the misappropriation of geophysical maps from Gulf Oil Company. Interestingly each of the defendants in these cases argued that no violation had occurred because the secret documents were copied and the originals returned to the files, therefore, the actual documents did not cross state lines. This argument was rejected, but it was left open whether federal law is violated when someone memorizes a secret formula and writes it down after crossing the state line.

The federal Mail Fraud Statute prohibits use of the United States Mail for the purpose of executing any "scheme or artifice to defraud." Two important questions must be affirmatively answered when reviewing a trade secret theft for prosecution under the Mail Fraud Statute:

(1) Was the theft used as an artifice or scheme to defraud?

(2) Did the theft use the mails to further the misappropriation?

Under the typical theft of trade secrets case involving a wrongful employee, the employer is defrauded of confidential information and also the confidential relationship and trust of the employer. These elements have been held to be sufficient to satisfy the fraud requirement of the Mail Fraud Statute.

The second requirement, use of the mails, has been satisfied in cases where the mailings were incident to an essential part of the scheme or where the use merely furthered the scheme. An example is the misappropriating employee's receipt of payment through the United States Mail, forwarded by the competitor after the theft was accomplished.

Criminal sanctions under state law require a specific review of the applicable state's criminal statutes. Several states, including California, Massachusetts, Michigan, Minnesota, New Jersey, and Ohio, have statutes making the acquisition of trade secrets a criminal offense if acquired through bribery of an employee. The California Penal Code Section 499c, is illustrative:

Every person who promises or offers or gives or conspires to promise or offer to give, to any present or former agent, employee or servant of another a benefit as an inducement, bribe or reward for conveying, delivering or otherwise making available an article representing a trade secret owned by his present or former principal, employer or master,

... is punishable by imprisonment in the state prison, or in a county jail *not exceeding one year,* or by a fine not exceeding five thousand dollars, or by both such fine and such imprisonment.

Other states provide criminal sanctions for trade secret theft upon traditional crimes such as larceny, embezzlement, receiving stolen property, burglary, and robbery. The criminal statute of New York illustrates a possible source of relief for a wronged trade secret owner.

New York Penal Law

§155.30 Grand larceny in the third degree

A person is guilty of grand larceny in the third degree when he steals property and when: ...

3. The property consists of secret scientific material ...

§165.07 Unlawful use of secret scientific material

A person is guilty of unlawful use of secret scientific material when, with the intent to appropriate to himself or another the use of secret scientific material, and having no right to do so and no reasonable ground to believe that he has such right, he makes a tangible reproduction or representation of such secret scientific material by means of writing, photographing, drawing, mechanically or electronically reproducing or recording such secret scientific material.

Criminal sanctions are effective legal weapons in trade secret warfare and should become an element of your contingency plan.

RICO—Racketeer Influenced and Corrupt Organizations Act

While RICO was designed primarily as a criminal statute, RICO does provide a private cause of action to any person injured in his business or property by reason of a violation of the federal statute. RICO is included in the trade secret arsenal of weapons because civil litigation under RICO provides treble damages for the prevailing plaintiff, costs, and a reasonable attorney's fee.

The threat of a RICO action, usually denoting an association with organized crime, can devastate the misappropriator's resistance to returning secret information or settlement. A good example of this remedy is IBM's settlement of an unfair competition, copyright infringement, and RICO action against Hitachi Ltd. in October of 1983. This action, primarily a civil RICO action, was instituted when

Hitachi's theft of IBM trade secrets was disclosed during a Federal Bureau of Investigation sting operation.

The elements of a Civil RICO action are illustrated by IBM's allegations contained in their complaint against Hitachi as follows:

62. Defendants are all associated with an enterprise engaged in interstate and foreign commerce. That enterprise is Hitachi or, in the alternative, an association in fact of the defendants.

63. The defendants have conspired to conduct and are conducting the affairs of the enterprise through a pattern of racketeering activity, consisting of repeated violations of 18 United States Code §§2314 and 2315 and applicable state laws, including commercial bribery laws. Those racketeering activities, resulting in the receipt of stolen IBM trade secrets, are used to generate profits for the enterprise and for each and every defendant.

64. IBM has suffered competitive injury as a result of the illegal advantage the defendants have obtained through their pattern of racketeering activity.

65. The defendants have violated the Racketeer Influenced and Corrupt Organizations Act, 18 United States Code §§1961-1968.

Claims under RICO are the latest weapons in trade secret protection warfare and complete the trade secret owner's arsenal. The threat of equitable, civil, and criminal retaliation in response to a trade secret theft provides a formidable deterrent. However, the primary goal remains the prevention of disclosure. This is best accomplished by preventive measures, i.e., contractual agreements, as detailed in the earlier chapters.

Conclusion

A well-prepared legal contingency action plan can stop a perpetrator in his tracks. If the existence of such a plan is accurately presented to your employees, it can be the greatest potential deterrent to internal trade secret theft. There should be no doubt in the minds of your employees or competitors that you will act immediately against anyone.

INDEX

A

Accountants, 91-92
Agents, 91
Antitrust laws vs. joint ventures:
   "Antitrust Guide Concerning Research
     Joint Ventures", 140
   EEC, 142
   foreign laws, 142
   National Cooperative Research Act of
     1984, 141
   new product, 141-42
   noncompetitive ventures, 141
   research and development, 140-41
Auditors, 91-92

B

Bankers, 90-91

C

Chain of responsibility in data control,
   162
Civil law countries, and trade secrets:
   legal effects, 177
   nature of common law in, 177
Collapse of negotiations, 121-23, 155
   competition, surveillance of, 123
   data banks, 122
   document return demand, 121-22
   follow-up, 122-23
   individuals to notify, 122
   third parties, 122
Common law countries, trade secrets in:
   court decisions as law basis, 176
   "stare decisis" doctrine, 176
Computers, trade secrets storage in,
   163-64
   screen, legend on, 163
Consultants, 49-50, 77. *See also*
   Outsiders
Copyright, 41
   and independent works, chance
     similarity of, 41
Corporate officers and directors, outsider
   company, 89-90
Courts, attitudes to trade secrets, 44-45.
   See also Litigation
   injunctions, 45
   judges, human reactions of, 45
   public policy conflicts, 44
   state laws, 45

Criminal sanctions, 214-17. *See also*
   Injunctions, Litigation
   California law, 215-16
   claim filing, 214
   Mail Fraud Statute, federal, 215
   New York State, 216
   Transport of Stolen Goods Statute,
     federal, 214-15

D

Damages: *See also* Litigation
   attorney's fees, payment of, 212-13
   bad faith, 213
   compensation, 211, 212
   disgorgement of profits, 212
   profit recovery, 212
   proving of, 211-12
   punitive, 213
   reasonable royalties, 212

E

EEC, trade secrets in:
   chemical manufacturers, 179-80
   disclosure, 179
   EEC Commission, 178
   France, 177, 180
   Germany, 180
   introduction of technology, 179
   Italy, 180
   royalties, 179
   secrets de commerce, 177, 180
   secrets de fabrique, 177, 180
   technology restriction, 179
   territorial restrictions, 179
Employees:
   education of on trade secret policies,
     164
   greatest threat of to trade secrets, 10
   hazards of in trade secrets:
     clerical personnel, 65
     corporate planning and marketing
       employees, 66-67
     custodial staff, 67
     deliberate actions of, 63-64
     ease of getting information, 63
     entrepreneurs, 64
     financial and operational employees,
       67
     high-level research personnel, 66
     leaving of job, 64
     mobility, 64

Employees *(cont.)*
  hazards of in trade secrets *(cont.)*
    technical and engineering support
        personnel, 66
    top executives, 65
    unintended disclosure, 63
  secrecy agreement:
    before employment, 71
    consideration in contracts, 72
    court attitudes to, 72
    description of trade secrets, 72
    example, 71
    needed elements, 72-73
    noncompetition covenant, 72
    state laws, 72
  update checks on after employment
      ends, 77-78
Employment interview, 69-70
  corporate policy on trade secrets,
      presentation of, 70
Exit interview, 75-77
  checklist, 76
  information to get, 76
  letter to send to former employee, 77
  signed affirmations in, 76
  use of to employer, 76
Export controls, United States, and trade
    secrets:
  banned countries, 174-175
  data, forms and types, 173
  export license, granting of, 174
  foreign company, approach by, 175
  foreign employees, 175
  military uses, 174
  public sources of data, 174
  purchase orders, wariness of, 175
  re-export, problem of, 174
  U.S.-owned subsidiary, trade secrets
      of, 175-76
  visitors, 175
Export Trading Company Act of 1982,
    142, 184-85

F

Financial institutions, 90-91
FOIA exemptions, mark to establish, 94
Future technology developments. *See*
    Grantbacks

G

Grantbacks, 99-102, 120. *See also entries*
    under License
  antitrust risks, scale of, 102
  definition of technology, 100
  grantback clause, 101
  option to future developments, 101
  payment for rights to, 101

H

High-technology companies:
  commercial life of trade secrets,
      brevity of, 189
  espionage, 192
  financial information, 191
  key employee risk, 190
  marketing information, 191
  military uses, 192
  outside suppliers and subcontractors,
      191-92
  protection, lack of, 189-90
  rapidly growing, 194-96
    hiring, problems with, 194-95
    innovation, 196
    and joint ventures, 196-97
    legal advice, problems with, 196
    outmoded systems for trade secrets
        control, 195
    related outside parties and trade
        secrets, 195-96
    sale, 196
High-technology employees:
  bias against administration, 193-94
  bias toward innovation, 193-94
  ignorance of legal mechanisms, 194
  mobility, 193
  short-term orientation syndrome, 194
  youth, 193
Hitachi/IBM case, 10, 217

I

Independent consultants, 92
Individual secrecy agreements, signing of
    in joint ventures, 162
Injunction, blitzkrieg techniques: *See also*
    Criminal sanctions
  ex-parte, 208
  preliminary, 207-08
  temporary restraining order, 208
  time limit, 208
International contracts:
  after-developed technology, ownership
      of, 184
  American businessmen, perspective on
      trade secrets, 171
  definition of trade secrets, 183
  disputes, resolution of, 184
  international markets, 172-73
  licensing outside United States, 172
  problem of which law applies, 183
  wholly-owned foreign subsidiaries, 172

J

Japan, 181-82
  in-kind trade, 181-82

Japan *(cont.)*
  injunctive relief, 181
  torts and damages, Civil Code, 181
Joint venture, control of, 158-59
  data control, 159
  number of partners in, 159
  unilateral voiding, 159
Joint venture, goals and scope in profile:
  attitudes, hazards of, 150
  bias, problems with, 147
  business reputation, 145
  damages, 153-54
  definition of trade secret information,
    150-51
  employees, identification of those with
    access, 151-52
  financial resources, 144-45
  inhouse staff to find, 146-47
  injunctive relief right, 153
  marketing, 145
  marking for documents, 152
  number of partners, 146
  outside consultants, 147
  prenegotiation secrecy agreement, 150
  quantification, 147-50
    profile chart, 148
  signing at high levels, 151
  technique for, 144
  time period for secrecy agreement,
    152-53
  who is bound, 151
Joint ventures, negotiating:
  employees' identification, 154-55
  information restrictions, 154
  periods to set, 154
  secrecy maintenance, 155
Joint ventures, developments during: *See
    also* Grantbacks
  residual rights, 166
Joint venture, premature termination of:
  buyout option, 167
  name of joint venture, 168
  new partners, finding of to replace, 168
  reasons for, 167
  valuation, 168
Joint venture, question of access to
    documents, 161-62
Joint venture, scope of trade secret use
    by, 160-61
Joint ventures, steps to end negotiations:
  confirmed receipt, 156
  difficult places to notify, 156
  formal documents for, 156
  future activities of partners, 158
  key individuals' notification, 156
  outside U.S., 156
  return time limit, 157

Joint ventures, steps to end negotiations
    (cont.)
  third party, formal notices, 157-58
  trade secret document protection, 157
Joint ventures, trade secrets of and
    outside parties, 164-65
Joint venture, and wholly-owned
    subsidiary, 161
Joint venturer, risks for:
  activities outside joint venture, 138
  after-developed technology, 137-38
  continuing obligation to disclose trade
    secrets, 136-37
  creation of competitors, 139
  discussion, 136
  employees of partner, 137
  expanding scope of, 138-39
  failure, price of, 139
  third parties, 137

K

Know-how, 39

L

Latin America, 182-83
Legal theories, 209-10
  express contract, 209
  torts, 209
  trade secrets as property, 209-10
License agreement:
  Act of God clause, 128
  consumer demand, 98
  cooperation of parties, 127
  cross-license, 97
  divisions, transfers of data between,
    124
  exclusivity, 125
  force majeure clause, 128
  future information transfers, 99
  grantbacks, 126-27
  identification of trade secrets, 126
  individual secrecy agreement, 126
  licensee's books and records, access to,
    127
  licensor as consultant, 125-26
  life of secrecy agreements, 128-29
  parent company as co-signor, 124
  parties to, 124
  rights assignment, 125
  short-term, 99
  termination clause, 128
  trade secrets acknowledgement, 124
  whereas clauses, 123-24
License term, trade secrets during:
  grantbacks, 129-30
  licensee's procedures, 129
  royalties, 129

Licensees, finding of:
  advantages of outside consultants, 107
  background information, 108-09
  data banks, 107
  elimination procedure, 112
  first contact, 112
  license prospectus, 109-10
    and licensor, 110
    preparation, 109
    products and technology, 110
    trade secrets to disclose, 110
  outside consultants, 107
  potential partners, range of, 111
  profile, quantification, 106
  rates charged, 108
  sections of companies, 108
  Suter Associates, 108
  trade secret notice, 109
Litigation against trade secret theft:
  criminal proceeding, 206
  damages, 205-06
    monetary, 206
    punitive, 206
  early detection, 202
  employees' morale in conflicts, 202
  injunctions, 204-05
    permanent, 205
    preliminary, 205
    temporary restraining order, 205
  litigation, effect on company, 202-03
  reputation, 202
  success in:
    chance of, 202-03
    damage, 204
    intent of misappropriator, 203-04
    proof needed, 203
    secrecy, degree of, 203
  trade secret disclosure, evaluation, 202

M

Maintenance, trade secrets:
  Chinese Wall syndrome, 119-20
  document list, 120
  internal conflicts, 119
  notices, 120
  prior notices of disclosure, 119
  secrecy control, 119

N

Negotiations. *See* entries under Joint
    Venture; License

O

Outsiders, agreement about trade secrets:
  affirmative obligations, 86-87
  components, 87
  designation of trade secrets, 85
  duration, 86

Outsiders, agreement about trade secrets
    (cont.)
  employees of, individual secrecy
      agreements, 87
  execution by all parties, 88
  liquidated damages, role, 88-89
  scope of disclosures, 85-86
  term of, 89
Outsiders, audit of trade secrets
    procedure, 164
Outsiders, risks of to trade secrets:
  approach to, 82-83
  assumptions to make, 83
  lack of consideration by, 82
  marks on documents, 81-82
  oral notification, 82
  warnings to, 81
Outsiders, submission of trade secrets by,
    92-93

P

Partners, potential, 92
Patents:
  commercial life, 26
  computer software, 24, 26
  in Constitution, 23
  disclosure for, 24
  disincentives, 40
  foreign costs, 25
  invalidation, 25
  legal definition, 39-40
  life of, 23
  original use, 23
  as property, 40
  requirements, 40
  risk, 23
  speed of technological advance, 24,
      40-41
  time to get, 24-25
  and trade secrets, 24
Permanent injunction, 211. *See also*
    Litigation
Planned termination of joint venture, 168
Post-employment consultation, 77
  continuing secrecy agreement, 77
Pre-employment screening procedures:
  activities of potential employee, 68
  financial standing, 69
  references, 69
  résumé evaluation, 68
Preliminary injunction, elements needed:
    See also Injunctions
  example, 210-11
  irreparable harm, 210
  opposing party, 210
  public interest, 210
Protection for trade secrets, program:
  accountability, 56
  classification, 53-54

Protection for trade secrets, program
 (cont.)
 corporate employee, 50
 critical information, 54
 document marking, 56
 employees, 57, 58, 59
  developments by, 58-59
 information, types of in firm, 50-53
 know-how, 55
 locating of, 50-51
 mechanical procedures, 57
 other data, 53
 outside consultant, 49-50
 periodic updates, 59
 physical isolation, 55-56
 reasons for, 49
 reinventing-the-wheel syndrome, 49
 sales and marketing personnel, 50
 technical information, 51-52
 third parties, 57-58
 tracking of custody, 56
 unsolicited submission of proprietary
  information, 58
Punishment for trade secret violators:
 deterrence, 201
 frightfulness policy, 201
 policy development, 201-02

R

Racketeer-Influenced and Corrupt
 Organizations Act, 216-17
Royalties, 129, 212

S

Sales representatives, 91
Secrecy agreements in licensing:
 conduct, 115
 defining of information, 113
 employee secrecy agreements, 115
 evaluations, 113
 large licensees, problems with:
  clause needed, 114
  divisions of, 114
  high-rank personnel, 114
 liquidated damages, 116
 period of validity, 115-16
 pre-negotiation requirement, 112-13
 time of signing, 113
 trade secret document marking, 116-17
 violators, injunctive relief, 116
 who should sign, question of, 114
Secrecy, general topics:
 bonds, 38
 confidential disclosure agreement, 38
 in corporation, 36-37
 failure of, 36
 joint ventures, 38-39
 public, 38
 and outside parties, 37-38

Secrecy, general topics *(cont.)*
 salesmen, 36
 supervision in secret phase, 38
 technology licensing, 38-39
Subcontractors, 90
Suppliers, 90
Suspect of theft of trade secrets:
 compensation, 74
 criminal action, 74
 discharge of, 74-75
 injunction, 74
 proofs, 74
 use of secrets, 75

T

Technical phase negotiations:
 ban on talk about trade secrets, 121
 continuing advice, 121
Third party secrecy agreement: *See also*
 Secrecy
 custody chain, 83
 employees, 84
 enforceability, 84
 in court, 83
 trade secret disclosure, 84
 who should sign, 83-84
Trade secrets, defining in joint venture,
 159-60
Trade secret documents, places for,
 162-63
Trade secrets, general topics:
 as corporate assets, 33-34
 legal establishment of, 34
 legal value, 34
 novelty of, 34
 range of, 9
 secrecy, 35-36
 states, differences between about, 33
Trade secrets, items to view as:
 corporate documents, internal, 43
 correspondence, 43
 customer information, 43
 financial and accounting data, 43-44
 formulations, 42
 industrial processes, 42
 legal issues, 44
 machinery, 42
 modifications, 42
 planning and strategy data, 44
 products, 42
Trade secrets, joint ventures' dealing
 with, 161
Trade secrets, and negotiations, 117-18.
 See also Joint ventures
 financial matters, 117
 high-level decision makers, 118
 personnel matching, 117
Trade secrets, vs. patents and copyrights,
 45-46

Trade secrets, recovery of: *See also*
    Litigation
  information return, 206-07
  litigation, protecting secrets in, 207
  writ of attachment, 207
Trading of secrets, license types:
  application descriptions, 118
  scope, problems with, 118
  tax laws, 118-19
Transactions, stages of:
  choice of licensee, 103-04
  corporate makeup, 104-05
  factors, 103
  financial resources, 104
  licensee, abilities of, 106

Transactions, stages of *(cont.)*
  location of, 105-06
  physical size, 104-05
  profile of licensee, 104
  technical competence, 106

U

Updates for employees, 73
U.S. Government, submission of data to,
  93-94

V

Venture capital lender, 91